EVERYTHING YOU NEED TO KNOW TO BECOME A PET PSYCHIC

About the Author

Photo credit: Alice Jeavons

Elizabeth (Beth) Lee-Crowther has been a professional animal communicator, pet psychic, psychic medium and reiki master for over 20 years. She regularly teaches animal communication workshops and hosts live demonstrations.

Beth's professional background includes working as an NNEB-qualified nursery nurse, running her own saddlery retail business and gaining numerous counselling qualifications. She believes that it is these career experiences that have given her a greater understanding of people and animals.

Beth regularly features on TV, radio and podcasts all over the world. Her first book, *Life by Numbers*, is an Amazon bestseller. She currently resides, with her partner Nigel, in the beautiful spa town of Malvern in Worcestershire, UK. Beth and her family have four rescue dogs that she loves to walk over the glorious Malvern Hills.

Connect with Beth:
psychicbeth.com
Instagram: elizabethleecrowther_psychic
Facebook: Psychic Beth
Facebook: Animal Communication and Pet Psychics

EVERYTHING YOU NEED TO KNOW TO BECOME A PET PSYCHIC

How to Master the Secrets of Animal Communication

Beth Lee-Crowther

Published in 2022 by Welbeck Balance
An Imprint of Welbeck Non-Fiction Ltd
Part of Welbeck Publishing Group
Based in London and Sydney.
www.welbeckpublishing.com

A CIP catalogue record for this book is available from the British Library

ISBN
978-1-80129-077-7

Typeset by Lapiz Digital Services
Printed Great Britain by CPI Group (UK) Ltd, Croydon CRO 4YY

10 9 8 7 6 5 4 3 2 1

Note/Disclaimer

Welbeck Balance encourages diversity and different viewpoints. However, all views, thoughts, and opinions expressed in this book are the author's own and are not necessarily representative of Welbeck Publishing Group as an organization. All material in this book is set out in good faith for general guidance; Welbeck Publishing Group makes no representations or warranties of any kind, express or implied, with respect to the accuracy, completeness, suitability or currency of the contents of this book, and specifically disclaims, to the extent permitted by law, any implied warranties of merchantability or fitness for a particular purpose and any injury, illness, damage, death, liability or loss incurred, directly or indirectly from the use or application of any of the information contained in this book. This book is not intended to replace expert medical or psychiatric advice. It is intended for informational purposes only and for your own personal use and guidance. It is not intended to diagnose, treat or act as a substitute for professional medical advice. The author and the publisher are not medical practitioners nor counsellors, and professional advice should be sought before embarking on any health-related programme.

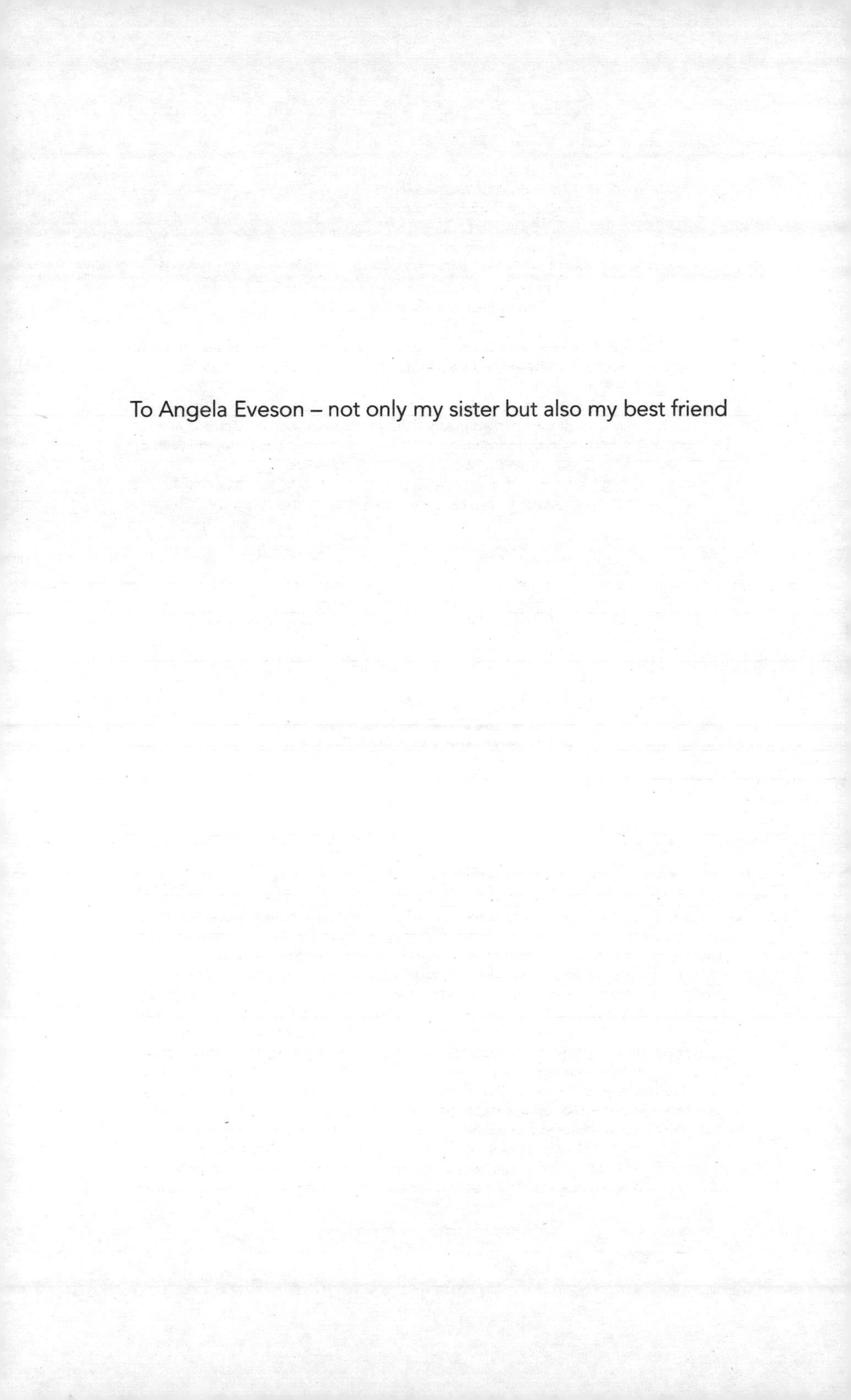

To Angela Eveson – not only my sister but also my best friend

Contents

Introduction

As a pet psychic and animal communicator, I am certain that animals, including our pets, are gifted healers who all have something important to teach us and significant lessons to share about how we choose to be in the world. I firmly believe, too, that humans are also intuitive beings and that we are all born with telepathic and psychic abilities.

As children, we let our imaginations lead us in our play and our games and as we form our relationships, but as we get older, we tend toward the logical in our lives and, as a result, our natural psychic abilities become stagnant through underuse. This does not mean that they no longer exist, or that we can no longer access them; it just means that they have been put on hold. Happily we can revive these extraordinary gifts, but just like a muscle that has become flabby through underuse, they need to be exercised to become stronger.

I have now spent many years exercising my own innate psychic abilities and, in particular, those abilities that allow me to communicate with animals. In this book I will demystify just how I do that and show you how you can do it too. I believe most animal lovers have this same ability and that it just needs to be coaxed out. The purpose of this book is to share the skills and techniques that you can learn in order to communicate with your pets.

Once you release your own potential as a pet psychic and skilled animal communicator, you will better understand your animals – and they can better understand *you*.

Growing Up with Animals

Although I was born in a bustling British city (Birmingham), we were never far from the countryside, and so, for as long as I can remember, I've always had a passion for animals. My parents have told me that as soon as I could walk and talk, Dad would have to stop the car at the end of our road so that I could stroke the two horses that lived in a field there. I drove my parents mad begging for a pet and, when they finally caved in, Dad took me to a pet store to choose a rabbit. I could see a tiny black-and-white Dutch rabbit in the window with about 20 others. (It was the 1970s and so this was how pets were often put on display in the pet store.) I just knew, instinctively, that the black-and-white one was mine. I rejected each one that the store assistant lifted up for me to consider until finally she got to "my" rabbit. It was as if I could hear his voice saying, "Choose me." I called him Benji, and we were best friends for 12 years. Benji was the first important animal in my life, but he was followed by many more: guinea pigs, cats, dogs, horses, ponies and even parrots.

As a young child I was obsessed with horses and rode ponies at a local stables. I dearly wanted a pony of my own, but that was a costly luxury and one that was out of our financial reach. When I was around 11, I was riding a small white pony called Toby when I realized I felt a sense of complete freedom and serenity. It was almost as though I'd stepped out of time and into a bubble of complete happiness, totally at one with my four-legged friend.

In my mind, I spoke with Toby, silently asking him questions in my head, and he would answer me in the pictures and words he sent back into my mind, telling me all about his past, including his previous injuries and his current aches and pains. To be honest, I thought this was normal – just something that happened when you rode horses. It wasn't until I asked a friend who was riding with me what her pony was saying, and saw her astonished expression, that I realized not everyone experienced what I did.

The Animal Communicator

It was to be another decade or more before I finally bought my own pony, Amberleigh. I was 23. This was just the start of my equine journey – many more horses and ponies were to follow. I talked to them all, just as I had talked to Toby, and they all talked back. We understood each other. I stayed around horses by starting my own saddlery business, providing tack and equipment both locally and online, and as people talked to me about their horses, I'd recommend the equipment they should try to best help them with whatever issue they were experiencing.

I already knew and felt confident that I could communicate easily with my own horses. But I wasn't sure whether I could communicate with other people's pets. So, I set out to test myself. I started by asking people for photos of their horses, and as I looked at the image, I'd find myself telling the owner all about their pet's background, their likes and their dislikes. I could even tune in to the root cause of any behavioural issues. Time and again, I was proved right. Word got around and people started coming to me, not just for the saddlery business, but with photos of their pets for me to "read". I became known in local animal circles as the pet psychic or the animal communicator.

My next challenge to myself was to see if I could do the same thing further afield. I reached out to people across the globe – primarily in the USA, France and Belgium and other places where I could not possibly have any prior knowledge of the animal – and asked owners to send me pictures of their pets. I was testing myself yet again and seeking proof that the only way I could know this information was from the animals themselves. I would sit with a photograph of the person's pet, close my eyes and then write down any impressions that came into my mind. Examples of this could be the characteristics and personality of the animal, its likes and dislikes, where it came from and its current home life, plus any health or behavioural issues. I would then email this information to the owner. The results were astounding, the findings being validated again and again.

I now had all the proof I needed and made the decision to accept this gift, at which point my life completely changed. I was so convinced that animals could send telepathic messages that I started to help people locate lost and missing animals. I was asked to track a missing dog, which led to me appearing on the local television news. As a result of that coverage, I was involved in a television documentary on missing and stolen animals and that led to multiple appearances on national TV in the UK.

Sharing My Skills

By then I knew animal communication was a real phenomenon, and I wanted to spread the word so that more and more people would understand that their animals can communicate with them if they learn how to hear what they are saying. I remember watching a film called *The Secret* which promised that the universe would fulfil your desires, but you had to ask. So, with some trepidation I asked the universe *how* I could spread the word.

Less than two weeks later, I was contacted by a DJ on a local radio station. I'd parked my car outside his house when attending a birthday party nearby and he had seen the sign advertising my services in my car window. I went on his show, and we were inundated with calls. It seemed everyone wanted to know what their pet was thinking. And it seemed the universe had heard me.

For the last 12 years I have been fortunate enough to have my own radio show, *The Spiritual Calling Show*. It started on a local UK radio station but is now on the *Pulse Talk Radio* platform so you can hear it from anywhere in the world. I have interviewed many leading mediums, psychics, therapists and animal communicators in the UK, and it has been a privilege to meet them all.

Can You Learn to Be a Pet Psychic?

Having heard more about how I got started as a pet psychic, you are probably now asking yourself, "Could I do this?" With very few exceptions, the answer is most certainly, "Yes."

And you really only need two key qualities: an open mind and a love of animals – that's it. Anyone who has these two attributes can undertake my training and learn to develop their intuition. And don't be surprised to learn that a healthy dose of scepticism is no bad thing. That is what made me constantly test myself – as I still do – by pushing at the boundaries of my psychic practice to expand my understanding and my psychic skills. Setting high standards for yourself is a way of ensuring that you maintain the quality of your work.

Of course, some people find the training easier than others. Having worked with so many people in the field, I've noticed how we all seemed to have shared the same experience as a child of feeling that we were different, and of having, at some point, a moment we would all describe as being one of "spiritual awakening". For some, it may even have been a near-death experience that convinced them of their special gift. I believe such awakenings are simply reminders of our spiritual selves. But if you have not experienced any such event in your life, that does not mean that you don't possess psychic ability, it simply means that it has remained dormant. People who make great pet psychics and animal communicators will probably identify with at least some of the following characteristics.

- You were often told as a child that you had a vivid imagination.
- You often feel that you are very different from other people.
- You relate to animals at least as easily as people.
- At times, you have experienced feelings that you just don't fit in.

- You love your pets as much as people and consider them to be members of the family.
- You may have faced some difficulties with personal relationships.
- You are interested in creative subjects.
- You have an appreciation for the arts and music.
- You occasionally worry about what others think of you.
- You empathise with others or "feel" their pain.
- You tend to overthink things or find it hard to switch off.

If you can identify with several of these then you are an ideal candidate to explore this fascinating subject and may even find it easier to trust your intuition than someone else who does not relate to these feelings.

What Will You Learn?

The more you know about a person, the more you understand how they think and feel and what is unique about them, and the same is true of pets. People adore their pets and want to give them the best possible life, but we must all be conscious that each animal is an individual with their own personality, agenda and purpose. This knowledge is both useful and enlightening, not only when it comes from animals who are well and happy but also from those ones who are experiencing illness, behavioural issues, emotional problems or trauma. It allows us to have a deeper understanding of our animals' specific needs (not the needs we think or assume they have) and gives us a better insight into the way they are behaving – and, more importantly, the reasons why.

Often, you will find that animals have important messages for us too. I have discovered they are not only aware of what is going on in our lives currently but they often also know, psychically, about past events that may still be affecting us, and they will know when we are facing difficulties of some kind. Your animals have so much to share, not just about themselves, but about you and your loved ones too. They can even help you discover your purpose in life, see what your future holds and make predictions about your life, as well as their own. This can be not only informative but a truly enlightening experience. As an owner you may well start to see your pet in a whole new light afterwards and find this has made the special bond between you even stronger.

Whatever the reason for your interest in learning more about being (and becoming) a pet psychic, you will discover something of great value in this book to help you learn and grow. In fact, you will learn as much about yourself as the animals you live with. And, as I've said, you do not require any previous experience or knowledge, just a willingness to learn.

It is important to learn new things so that we can progress and grow through life, but in order to do that you will be required to step out of your comfort zone. This may feel a little bit alarming at times, but I am asking you to trust me and trust this process. Taking this risk will enable you to better develop your own intuition and to explore your own inner guidance too, so don't be surprised if you get to the end of the book and find that you see the world in a whole different and more enriching way.

About this Book

As my own abilities grew, I was thrilled by my new-found psychic skills, but I understood the importance of staying real and grounded. To this day, I never take anything for granted, and I appreciate and honour the gifts I have been blessed with. I am also committed to sharing them with anyone open-minded enough to give it a go, and to achieve that, I developed my Animal Communication and Psychic Development Workshops.

This book will share all the information I taught on those courses. Through this book, you too will be able to communicate with your pets, as long as you stay open-minded and are willing to put in a little practice. Remember, muscles need to be exercised!

I have divided this book into three parts. To start, we will look at the different types of animal communication; I will explain what being a pet psychic entails and how we can receive messages from our pets. You will see how these different types of communication are used in different situations as we progress through the book.

I will then move on to the "How To" part of the book. First, we will look at the most effective techniques that form the basis for all animal communication. I will show you how to get into a state of relaxation so that you are ready to hear from your pet. Then, you will learn the necessary skills to undertake a reading, and how to open and close a reading. This chapter also contains exercises to help you develop your own psychic skills. Repeating these fundamentals will strengthen your new psychic training knowledge and gradually be overlaid with subtle layers of understanding that deepen your psychic practice.

Throughout the book I have included Animal Profiles – these are practice exercises for you to test yourself as your confidence as an animal communicator grows.

Start this journey with me now, and together we will open up a whole new world of loving communication and deeper understanding between you and your pet.

Author's Note

This book is for all animal lovers who want to understand the animals in their lives better by learning how to communicate with them more meaningfully. It is not a book about treating sick pets or a substitute for a visit to the vet if that is what is needed, although it will introduce you to the idea that you can do much to keep your animal well with both hands-on and remote healing. If your veterinary practice is sympathetic to more holistic forms of animal healing, you may, of course, wish to share your thoughts and findings about your animal's current state of wellness with those qualified practitioners or others who may have an involvement with your animal, including trainers, behaviourists, groomers and, if you work or go on holiday, your day-care sitters.

PART 1

Understanding Animal Communication

Here, we will explore in detail the different types of animal communication you will learn through this book: telepathy, psychic connection and mediumship.

Take time to reflect on these types of communications and make sure you're clear on the differences between them. As we look at different situations and readings later in the book, you'll see these three types in action.

1

What Is Animal Communication?

To begin communicating with your pet, you will need to first understand what we mean by animal communication, how it works and what the difference is between the three main types that I teach. These are telepathic communication, psychic communication and mediumship. This basic groundwork will give you the firm foundation you will need to move on and learn about my Psychic Animal Communication Technique (or PACT as we'll refer to it from now on), and to then begin to put your new-found psychic skills into practice with the animal or animals that you love.

How Animals Communicate with Each Other

Animals communicate with each other through many different means by using signals and cues, including visual, auditory, touch, smell, pheromones and behaviour. This communication can take place within their own species but also with other species, including humans. Common behaviours and body language can encompass posture, gestures, facial expressions, changes to the lie of their coat and eye contact. Other behaviours may be species-specific.

- **Dogs** typically mark their territory by urinating. The urine contains chemicals and pheromones that tell other dogs through smell who has been that way. Dogs wag their tails when they are happy, drop to a submissive posture and look away when scared, and growl when aggressive.
- **Cats** wave their tails to show displeasure; they purr and knead a soft surface when they are happy.
- **Horses** often groom each other by biting each other's necks and backs. This helps create social bonds.
- **Monkeys** pick insects off each other in mutual grooming and bare their teeth to show displeasure or aggression.
- **Birds** use their beaks for many different reasons, not just for eating. They may bite if they are defending their territory or feeling fearful. Birds can also play by grabbing each others' beaks. They sing, chirp, whistle and fluff their feathers to communicate with potential mates or to show they feel threatened. Some species, such as parrots, can repeat words or phrases and imitate sounds they hear.
- **Fish and aquatic animals** can transmit sound waves through water. Scientists have even identified individual fish songs used to communicate with others of the same species; e.g. a cod will sing the cod song.
- **Dolphins** exhibit many sophisticated sounds including clicking and whistling to communicate with each other.

Each of these gestures or actions has a meaning – just as words do – which convey how the animal is thinking or feeling. They also convey their intentions toward other creatures. Certain behaviours are used to attract or accept a mate, to establish a social hierarchy, to show submission or superiority, to display anger or friendship, to warn of danger or show they want to fight.

How Animals Communicate with Humans

Animals largely use these same methods to communicate with us. (Interestingly, cats only seem to meow at humans, not to other cats!) So, whether you have a dog, cat or any other animal, you will be familiar with these different ways of communicating, and probably many more. You will already be adept at recognizing these signals and understanding what the animal is experiencing and its mood. The more we get to know our pets, the more we deepen this understanding of the unique ways our animals have of telling us what they want. My Jack Chi dog, Tilly, for example, scratches my leg until I give her a bite of my meal. My parrot, Marty, would make the sound "ooooh" if he wanted a food treat. If we observe closely we can easily learn the signals animals use instinctively to communicate with their own species. This means we can then start to interpret what they are trying to tell us and adapt our own communication methods accordingly.

How Humans Communicate with Animals

Anyone who loves and perhaps works with animals – such as horse whisperers, dog behaviourists, pet groomers, dog handlers and vets – are natural animal communicators. They recognize the signals animals rely on to communicate and can respond to them intuitively. Often, animal lovers mimic natural behaviours. You may crouch down and make yourself smaller when approaching a timid dog, or avoid eye contact with an angry one, for example.

If you respond in a particular way every time your pet exhibits a certain behaviour, then this reinforcement teaches them that if, for instance, they snuggle up against your leg and put their head on your lap, they'll get a cuddle. They will also recognize actions you take and respond to them. You may have noticed that your dog gets excited as soon as you go to lift their lead off the hook. But once you have become a true animal communicator, they will get just as excited when you are simply thinking about taking them for a walk! Animals can also anticipate our arrival home. They will become excited and often look through the window or wait at the front door minutes before we walk up the path.

Animals acknowledge our physical stance, body language and gestures, too, and we use this when training them. A firmly pointed finger, bending down to them or offering an open hand for them to sniff all convey an important meaning from us to them.

Of course, we also use language to communicate with our pets. Animal lovers talk to their pets all the time. As well as telling them it's time for dinner or a walk, we may tell our pets our problems and even our plans for the day ahead. I often tell my dogs when I'm popping out to the shops and how long I will be.

Pets will soon learn the specific words we use and the tone associated with them. One of the first things they learn is their name. Repetition reinforces the meaning. If you listen to the way you say specific words – "walkies", "sit", "good boy", "bad dog" – you will know exactly the cadence and tone you use each time, and so will your pet. Some commands have become common, such as "woah" to tell a horse to slow down or stop, or "walkies" to indicate we are taking a dog for a walk, but it is likely you also already have your own commands that are specific to your pet.

EXERCISE

What We Can Learn from Animals

Animals are teachers. They teach us about patience, understanding, compassion, working together, forgiveness, support, assertiveness, resilience and unconditional love.

Sit quietly when you do this exercise and use a photo of your pet to help you, if you wish. Think about one of your pets; you can choose one who has passed away or one that is still with you.

What three important lessons have they taught you? You may receive this information as three separate words or phrases.

Do you and your pet have any personality similarities?

Did/does your pet ever stare at you as though they were trying to tell you something?

Go with the first thought that comes into your mind. Make a note of it.

This is the first step in communicating with animals.

This exercise highlights the bond you have shared with your pet. It starts off the process of relaxing the mind, enabling thoughts to pass to and fro, from your mind to theirs and vice-versa. It gives you the opportunity to examine the relationship between you and your pet. Giving yourself the opportunity to do this exercise will help you reach an understanding of your own self awareness.

Animals as Holistic Healers and Helpers

Those of us who love animals already know that our pets respond to human emotions and will comfort us when we are sad and celebrate with us when we are happy. They pick up on our energy. If we are nervous or anxious, our pets often mirror this behaviour. If we are angry or afraid, our pets may demonstrate aggressive tendencies toward others. We can use this "mirroring" of our emotions to our advantage. Due to their sensitive nature and highly tuned senses, dogs are often given jobs to assist people. And other animals, such as horses, can also assist with all aspects of our health and wellness.

- **Medical alert assistance dogs** are trained to detect life-threatening health conditions, including problems associated with type 1 diabetes, severe allergies, epilepsy and even certain cancers.

- **Mobility assistance dogs** help those who are physically disabled by carrying out helpful tasks, such as opening and closing doors, picking things up and even turning on lights.
- **Guide dogs** support people with visual impairment so that they can be independent in their day-to-day lives, in and out of the home.
- **Hearing dogs for the deaf** alert deaf people to important sounds and lead them to the source or away from danger.
- **Animal-assisted therapy dogs** offer emotional support to sick or injured people. Often, they visit patients in hospital or residents in a care home environment. They can also be used in schools for anxious students.
- **Riding for the disabled** charities provide equestrian therapy to riders of all ages and with varying disabilities. This includes horseback riding and carriage driving. It enables a freedom of movement that those taking part may otherwise never experience and has many therapeutic benefits which are now recognized by medical professionals. Benefits include improving co-ordination and strengthening core stability. Riding also offers the chance to regain mobility and to experience a sense of real achievement by attaining realistic goals.
- **Equine-assisted therapy** has been developed in order to counsel people and help them to understand and deal with their issues, traumas and even addictions. It works by encouraging participants to carry out horse-care tasks,

such as leading or grooming, and then to work alongside a horse and its expert horse handler, facing and overcoming obstacles together. See page 214 for more on this.

Now we've looked at the everyday way that animals communicate with us and each other, let's move our focus to the deeper connection that we are trying to achieve.

In the next chapter, we'll look at the different ways in which we communicate mind-to-mind with an animal and, in doing so, gain the kind of information that is normally unknowable and develop conversations that are normally unachievable.

2

How I Communicate with Animals

In animal communication, we take the notion that we can mimic natural communication behaviours and energy, and we build on that to better understand our pets and help them to understand us. This means animal communication really is a natural connection between your mind and that of your pet or another animal. It is completely non-verbal — a direct transfer of information from a human mind to an animal mind and vice versa. In my work, I use three types of animal communication, which have similarities but also subtle differences.

- **Telepathic communication** is mind-to-mind communication between a human and an animal to discover how they think and feel.
- **Psychic communication** is similar to telepathic communication but with the addition of an ability to remember the past and see the future.
- **Mediumship** is also a form of psychic communication but it involves talking with the spirit world, either human or animal, to get more information.

The first thing to understand is that all three of these methods work very differently from what we think of as "normal" communication. In telepathy and psychic communication we are working directly mind-to-mind. What is different is that this type of communication enables us to look at a situation from an animal's perspective and understand things from their point of view. Animal professionals often describe having an "inner knowing" about an animal or a feeling about a behavioural issue or a health problem, which often turns out to be correct. This demonstrates the natural intuitive ability that they possess.

Let's look more closely at what these three different psychic communication methods are and explore what they involve and how they are used, before learning how to put them into practice ourselves.

Telepathic Communication

Telepathy is a form of extrasensory perception, also known as ESP, which allows an individual to know what another is thinking or feeling without verbal communication and without using any other physical signs. This is just how I communicated with Toby, the pony.

Many people believe that humans only use a small proportion of their brain power – some estimates put this at 15% or less – so we don't fully understand how the whole brain works, but scientific experiments are advancing the boundaries of knowledge and actually demonstrating that telepathic transfer is possible, not just fanciful. We have yet to unlock the potential of the remaining percentage of the brain's power, so it is perfectly feasible that we will eventually be able to prove how telepathy works at a scientific level.

Telepathy is often explained as a mind-to-mind connection that works by tapping into the other person's energy fields. Our brain gives out messages via electrical signals, which can be transmitted and then received and interpreted by someone else. You have most likely encountered telepathy in your daily life. For example, have you ever thought about someone and just a few moments later they phoned you?

Serious scientists who have studied telepathy and animal communications and published papers in the field include the respected British biologist Rupert Sheldrake, who is the author of over 90 scientific papers and nine books, including a series of papers called *Unexplained Powers of Animals*. In his book *Dogs That Know When Their Owners Are Coming Home* (Arrow Books, 2000), Sheldrake states that:

> *"We and our pets are social animals linked together by invisible bonds, connecting animals to each other, to their owners and to their homes in powerful ways."*

In 1999, this book won the Scientific and Medical Network Book of the Year award.

Psychic Communication

Psychic communication adds another layer of connection to the telepathic one. A pet psychic will establish an energetic link between themselves and the animal which allows them not only to share the animal's thoughts and feelings but also access other areas of their knowledge. I believe animals have an acute sixth sense and that your pets know a lot about your life. Animals seem to be able to see into our souls; in my pet psychic readings I have passed many messages on to the owner from their pet. Pets can talk about things that we have encountered in the past, as well as our present circumstances, and they also seem to know about the challenges we may face in our future.

DAISY, THE GERMAN SHEPHERD

A German Shepherd dog called Daisy communicated to me that Lizzie, her owner, would get pregnant and have a daughter within a year. But since Lizzie never wanted to have children and had no plans to start a family, she just laughed when I told her. Just a few weeks later, however, she messaged me to tell me she had discovered she was pregnant; she went on to have a baby girl. Lizzie was shocked yet delighted and amazed that Daisy had made this prediction – so amazed, in fact, that the new mum attended one of my workshops in order to experience communicating with Daisy herself.

Mediumship

Mediumship has been described as the ability to communicate beyond the limits of the physical world with either animals or humans who have passed on to the spirit world. So, some mediums are animal communicators, and they will use a psychic connection that crosses the boundaries of this life into the next. I have witnessed many mediumship demonstrations where the medium not only describes a person who has passed away but also the animals that are in the spirit world with them.

Being Open to All the Options

Some practitioners use telepathy, others use psychic connections or mediumship, others all three. There can often be a natural progression between them because animal communicators are already open-minded and have learnt to access an altered state of mind. I use all three categories in my work, and you'll find yourself switching between – or combining – the types of communication depending on the situation.

Before we look at each in more depth, I just want to say that, while I focus mainly on dogs, cats and horses in this book (because these are the animals people most commonly ask me to communicate with), I believe we can communicate with every animal in this way, as I have done with small mammals, reptiles, farm animals, wildlife, zoo animals, birds, insects, fish and aquatic animals, including dolphins and whales.

As long as they are willing to do so, my experience is that all animals have this ability to communicate mind-to-mind, and it has nothing to do with higher intelligence, which means you really can use my techniques to communicate with any species of animal.

In the following chapters, we'll look at each type of communication in turn. Make sure to absorb this information fully and reflect on each technique. They'll appear throughout the book, so a good understanding of them now will be a big help later on!

3

Telepathic Communication

The first method I want to explore in depth with you is telepathy. I can't emphasize enough that anyone is capable of this type of communication with their pets, and while you may feel your innate abilities have faded since childhood, I will show you how – with guidance, practice and commitment from you – your telepathic skills can be reactivated.

Telepathic communication will work with any animal, at any time and over any distance. You do not have to be in the same room or space as the animal to conduct a reading or telepathic session. You can do it just by looking at a photograph of the animal. What this shows is that this kind of transfer of information is not based on any observations of an animal's body language or behaviour – as in the more common communication methods we all know and use – and so it really can be practised on animals you know nothing about.

Many people communicate telepathically with their pets without realizing it. You are probably doing this, too. I'm going to help you unlock the process and show you how you can hear what your pet is thinking. The secret to being able to hear the animal's thoughts is to trust what comes into your mind. The process is mind-to-mind. It requires some concentration and focus from you, but try to stay in an easy and relaxed state because this is not something you can or should force.

Sending and Receiving

When you are in telepathic communication with an animal, you are connecting directly with their mind, which means you will see and feel precisely what that animal is at that precise moment. You may receive messages via all of your senses during a reading, as well as experience strong feelings, thoughts and emotions. You need to stay open and observe what comes into your mind.

It is possible, too, for you to send messages to the animal in exactly the same ways. As mentioned, in order to achieve this transfer of energy, you need to be in a relaxed state, both physically and mentally, which will allow these thought messages to flow in both directions between you. I will show you the basics of how to achieve this in chapter 7.

Why Use a Telepathic Reading?

Typically, a telepathic reading with an animal communicator will take between 30 minutes and 1 hour. The animal may or may not be present because you can read from a photograph or even from a physical description of the animal; all you will need is the animal's name, breed, colour and markings.

You might choose to use a telepathic reading for a number of reasons:

- To help understand the root cause of a behavioural issue.
- To help understand the root cause of an illness and find out more about any pain or discomfort the animal is experiencing.
- To discover your animal's likes and dislikes, including food, people, bedding, environment and activities.
- To prepare the animal for imminent changes, such as a house move, a change in ownership, a family member moving out or the arrival of a new baby or a new pet.
- To help heal previous trauma, including grief, neglect and abuse, shock or injuries.
- To assist with work or performance, including show ring performance and the work of animals such as police dogs or assistance pets.
- To resolve potential issues to help your pet cope on long car journeys, when travelling by public transport or before travelling in horseboxes.
- To better understand a rescue animal's history and background so that they can be settled into a new home successfully.
- To locate lost or missing pets.

SMORTS, THE RAT

Sue was worried about her pet rat Smorts because his brother, Smurphy, had passed away, so she wanted to know how he was feeling.

During the communication, Smorts made me feel very emotional. It was apparent that he was aware of the passing of his brother and was grieving, just like his owner. Sue was keen to know if Smorts would be okay on his own without his brother.

Smorts showed me through images in my mind that he had a strong bond with his owner and that he loved to spend time with her and enjoyed being handled. Sue confirmed this. I telepathically asked Smorts if there was any message that I could pass on to Sue. He communicated to me that the bedding in his cage had been dusty and had made him feel uncomfortable and affected his breathing.

After sharing this information with Sue, she said it was amazing as the vet had also told her to change the type of bedding, which she had just done. Smorts also shared that he needed his water changing to filtered water, which Sue agreed to do. Then he showed me a mental image of his teeth needing attention. Sue got them checked by the vet and discovered he had indeed got dental problems.

Sue was very grateful for this communication and said it really helped her understand not only how Smorts was feeling, but also how she could make him more comfortable.

Each animal communicator finds their own unique way of working and you, too, will discover your own strengths and abilities as you gain a deeper understanding of the subject. There is no right or wrong way.

We will look in detail at my own method of carrying out a telepathic reading in chapter 9.

BIANCA, THE WHITE MARE

A few years ago, when I had the privilege of owning horses, I would experiment with the concept of telepathically communicating with them while riding. I stopped giving the usual verbal and physical commands to ask a horse to change pace from walk to trot or trot to canter or canter to gallop, and would merely think about going faster. My horse would then respond accordingly. I would also do this for slowing down or turning left or right and even stopping. Before long, it became normal for me to ride my horses in this way, and I believe it not only helped us develop a greater understanding of each other but also increased my riding ability and, therefore, my confidence.

Back in 1996 some friends of mine bred hardy Welsh ponies. They owned a white mare called Bianca – as stubborn as she was beautiful. Bianca had given birth to a very pretty foal of show quality and bloodlines. My friends were keen to enter the pair for the mare and foal classes at local shows. The problem was that Bianca flatly refused to go into a horsebox, causing a two- or three-hour delay while they tried to coax her in.

I had a soft spot for Bianca, even though she was cantankerous and awkward; I admired and respected her individuality. So, one day, when my friends wanted to take her to a show, I made a bet that I could load her into the horsebox in less than two minutes. They burst out laughing and said that it was impossible. But I knew that it wasn't stubbornness but fear that was making her refuse to go into the box. Bianca was afraid that if she entered a horsebox, she would be taken away from this home she loved and never return. This fear had built up because she had already moved home several times due to her challenging behaviour.

I telepathically communicated with her and promised she would return back home after the show. I told her she could trust me and that she should allow me to slowly and calmly walk her straight into the horsebox. She obliged while my friends looked on in disbelief. I had never told them about my animal communication abilities. I just told them that I had "my own methods" of persuasion. After that I was called on every time they wanted to take Bianca to a show, and it became a standing joke that I was the only person that she would allow to load her into the horsebox. I can safely say I won that bet!

4

Psychic Communication

A pet psychic can also be called a pet clairvoyant or sometimes a pet medium, but – strictly speaking – these terms refer so someone who communicates with both the living and those that have passed into the spirit world, and not all pet psychics work this way. We will look at the work of a pet medium in chapter 15, but here we will focus on working *psychically* with an animal.

While an animal communicator uses a conscious and telepathic mind-to-mind link between themselves and the animal, a pet psychic – while they may also use telepathy – establishes a psychic connection. This means a pet psychic can pick up more than just information about the animal itself. They can sense what the animal *knows* about its owner and shed light on significant events, not just those in the past and present but also things that may happen in the future too.

FRED, THE HORSE

On one occasion I was asked to carry out an animal communication reading by a lady named Caroline with her

horse, Fred, who was suffering from some back problems. Not only was Fred able telepathically to share information about the cause of his back problems, he also revealed some interesting information about his owner.

Fred predicted that Caroline would meet a new partner who would live in Devon. He said Caroline's new love would be tall with dark hair, would spend a lot of time on the water and would have a scar on his leg. This later proved to be true, as Caroline went on to meet Charlie, a sailor from Devon, who revealed he had a scar on his leg from a childhood operation. This seems like proof that animals can know about the future!

Forms of Psychic Reading

Psychic information from your pet can come in a variety of forms, notably clairvoyance, clairaudience, clairsentience and claircognizance. The prefix "clair" is French, meaning "clear".

Most pet psychics possess all these qualities, and you will discover that you almost certainly share at least some of them. Take note of anything that particularly resonates with you.

Clairvoyance

Clairvoyance literally means "clear seeing" and is often referred to as the "sixth sense" or the "third eye". It is the ability to see clearly into the non-physical. Clairvoyants report seeing intuitive pictures in their mind which can look both backward and forward in time.

Clairvoyants may practise divination: trying to ascertain the future by non-scientific means; these can include reading the pictures and patterns in tea leaves, seeing visions in a crystal ball or using cleansed crystals or their favourite oracle cards.

People who are clairvoyant may share particular characteristics; they often:

- Have a good imagination and are able to visualize things easily.
- Experience vivid dreams.
- Have a tendency to daydream.
- Are good at problem-solving.
- Are highly empathic, with the ability to see things from another's point of view.
- Enjoy storytelling in television, films and theatre.
- Have an attraction to colours and colourful clothing.
- Are very creative.

Clairaudience

This translates as "clear hearing", and those with this ability will often hear voices, sounds and even music within their mind and beyond the normal range of physical hearing. This often sounds like your own voice inside your head, similar to when you read or talk silently to yourself.

Clairaudients often:

- Love listening to music.
- Prefer learning through audio and listening.

- Enjoy listening to the radio and podcasts.
- Enjoy talking on the phone.
- Talk or mumble to themselves.
- Are good listeners.
- Hear their voice being called when no one is there.
- Offer good advice.
- Hear their own voice inside their head giving them advice.
- Experience ringing or other noises in the ears.

WHAT HAPPENS AT A PSYCHIC READING

If you were to attend a reading with a pet psychic, it would normally last between 30 minutes and one hour. The animal may be physically present, or the process can be carried out with a photograph or just a description. You might ask for a psychic reading for any of the reasons listed under the section on telepathic readings (page 19), but the scope of the messages may well be much broader.

Clairsentience

Clairsentience means "clear feeling". This relates to sensing emotions, feelings and even physical sensations through intuition. For instance, a clairsentient may pick up on another person's pain, emotional state or mood and will receive strong gut feelings about others.

People who are clairsentient often:

- Are described as "down to earth" by others.
- Appreciate being in nature and finding peace and quiet.
- Become overwhelmed in busy places.
- Have a sensitive nature and can become emotional.
- Show great empathy toward others.
- Have strong gut reactions about people and situations.
- Are aware of their environment and like to be surrounded with comfortable and cosy furnishings.
- Seek out similar people to spend time with.
- Are sensitive to the atmosphere within a room or building.

Claircognizance

Claircognizance translates as "clear knowing". This relates to having an "inner knowing" about another being, a place, an event or even an object and this knowledge being manifested as thoughts. It's about knowing when something or someone is true and authentic. It also relates to trusting our instincts. Claircognizant people recognize when someone is being sincere or not.

Claircognizant people often:

- Have a sense of "inner knowing" and knowledge.
- Often experience *déjà-vu* moments.
- Are good at problem-solving.
- Work well with their intuition.

- Have lots of ideas and inspiration.
- Show empathy toward other people's pain.
- Spend time thinking things through before acting upon their ideas.

As you begin your own psychic development journey through the practical exercises in this book, you will start to become more aware of these psychic qualities and preferences within yourself.

Before long, you will have identified which of the "clairs" you use to pick up your psychic information, and with practice you'll be able to expand on this.

TWO PARROTS CALLED MARTY

I have often communicated with birds (mainly parrots) and have even owned two African Greys, both called Marty.

The first Marty came to me from Ron and Carla when Carla was widowed and was no longer able to look after him. He was a grumpy boy and would often try to bite me, but he had his lovable side too. I communicated with Marty to ask if he was happy living with us and if he needed anything. He told me, very clearly, "I miss Ron," and showed me images of the two of them together. In one picture, Marty was inside Ron's coat with his head poking out the top. I asked Carla about this and she said that Ron would take Marty everywhere with him and carry him inside his coat. It was soon apparent that Marty did not like being handled by females, but he bonded quickly with my son, Kieran. Each time Kieran came home from work, Marty would shout out his name until Kieran paid him some attention. He was a very vocal bird and amused us with his range of vocabulary.

Marty was with us for three years before he passed away from old age; he was in his 50s! We were all devastated and I decided that I would let his cage and belongings go, as I had no intention of owning a parrot again. But a couple of days later I received a phone call from a lady called Verity. She said she had heard that I had recently lost a parrot and had tracked me down. She then revealed that Ron was her first husband and that they had purchased Marty together in the 1960s. After Ron had left, taking the original Marty with him, she had gone to buy a second parrot, also called Marty. Verity thanked me for taking care of the first Marty and then said that she had a huge favour to ask. She explained she was getting older, needed to go into hospital for an operation and was worried about what would happen to her Marty. "I need you to take Marty," she pleaded. Despite my surprise, I agreed to visit her to meet Marty (2) and, of course, I ended up bringing him home with me.

This Marty was in his late 20s and was shy and timid; a very different character from my Marty (1). Yet we developed a close bond, and he allowed me to handle him. Marty became instrumental in my animal communication workshops. He started to become more confident and enjoyed the attention from my students, who delighted in practising animal communication with him. I would get the students to ask him telepathically what his favourite food was, and they would often get the reply "banana", which he loved. One time a student called Sarah received a different reply to the favourite food question. She said that Marty had told her he liked potato chips, which was odd because I had never given him any. Curiosity got the better of me, so I went and bought a packet of the variety he had mentioned. I offered Marty one and, snatching it from my hand, he happily tucked in! I can only assume that Verity fed them to him as a treat.

I'm sharing this story because it makes the point that we must never assume we already *know* what an animal will communicate to us – even when it is an animal we think we know well. Learning to become non-judgemental and to not anticipate the animal's answers is an important skill to master as we develop our pet psychic muscle.

We owned Marty (2) for over ten years before he passed away following a short illness. I communicated with him after his passing, and he showed me an image of himself in flight. I heard the words, "I can fly". This gave me great comfort as, before I'd had him, his wings had been clipped so he'd been unable to fly. When we pass away we are no longer constrained by our physical bodies, and so Marty really was free. I still miss him greatly, and I will never forget the unexpected way he came into our lives.

5

Mediumship

Mediumship takes the non-physical psychic communication we have been exploring in the previous two chapters a step further: into the world of the spirit. And, if you have ever been to a mediumship demonstration, you will know that this is where the medium will describe a person or animal who has passed away and so is now in the spirit world.

Mediums are not usually specifically animal communicators, but if an animal who has passed wants to send a message to a beloved owner still living, they will find a way, so a medium may end up relaying messages from animals, as well as from relatives and friends who have died.

What Mediumship May Tell You about Your Pet

You might use mediumship for any of the same reasons listed under telepathy, but connecting via mediumship could go much deeper and also include:

- Communicating with an animal that has passed away.
- Giving validated information from your pet that only you understand, therefore proving the existence of life after death. This can be extremely comforting.
- Understanding the circumstances of how a pet passed away.
- Passing psychic messages from a deceased pet to a living owner – pets know a lot about their owners' lives and may predict future events.
- Offering guidance to owners. This will be in the form of messages that can help you or the owner to move forward with their grief or with problems or dilemmas.
- Making a connection to another animal that is known or has belonged to the owner.

A Second Visitor

Once you start developing and practising your animal communication skills and allow this psychic communication to take place, you will also be "open" to receiving other "visitors" that you may not have anticipated. I have attended mediumship evenings where the energy of an animal in spirit enabled the energy of a relative who had also passed to come through with messages. This may not be what was intended, but it is always a welcome surprise.

The important thing to remember is that none of this can happen unless everyone involved feels comfortable with it happening. This means there really is nothing to worry about and nothing to fear. Communication from "second visitors" will only happen if you want to work this way and when you are ready.

When you communicate with a pet that has passed, either directly or on behalf of someone else as part of a reading, you may find that you get messages from another pet with a connection to the owner – a childhood pet that has passed over, for instance, or even a pet that is currently in the household. Don't be thrown by this. You are simply opening the channels of communication and holding a safe space so that a pet can send a message to an owner and vice versa.

If you feel the energy change while communicating with a pet, it may be because you're picking up on the energy of another animal. If this happens, you can take a pause and ask this pet if it has a specific reason for showing up; listen carefully to what they tell or show you.

LUCY, THE DALMATIAN

Les and Gill explain:

In 2008 our precious Dalmatian, Lucy, was diagnosed with liver cancer; she passed away just before Christmas, leaving only our memory of her looking up at the Christmas lights on the tree with her mum, Perdy, and her brother, Ebony, beside her. We were totally devastated to lose her.

My wife and I were struggling with her passing when we found Beth; the picture showing Beth with three Dalmatians convinced us she was the right animal communicator for us.

We sent her a photo of us with all our dogs and arranged a reading over the phone.

Beth described Lucy's personality and manners perfectly and told us some very personal things that only we would know. We felt this gave us all the evidence we needed that Lucy had indeed made contact from the spirit world. We were really comforted by her words. Beth told us she could see me putting the urn which holds Lucy's ashes on my knee. This was true and is what happens. We take Lucy's ashes to our holiday home in Anglesey in Wales every time we go, and I carry her on my knee.

We had another encounter with Beth when we saw her sailing down the river on the *Lady Diana* cruise boat in Chester, England. She was there on a surprise trip from her home in Birmingham. As we waved to her from the bank, we realized we were standing at the exact spot where Lucy had had her last ever walk with us.

By 2015 our remaining dogs, Perdy and Ebony, were old and struggling, so we had them put to sleep together. We arranged another reading with Beth which, once again, brought us great comfort and peace of mind at a very sad time. We now take three lots of ashes to our holiday home and we are always comforted by the thought that our dogs really have gone to a beautiful place together.

My response:

Open-minded animal lovers often begin to see life in a different way and start noticing more signs and synchronicities. A common sign from loved ones who have passed away is seeing white feathers on the ground and robins close by. Owners Lesley and Gill recognized this when they first made contact with me about Lucy, their dog who had died. They believed my picture with three Dalmatians was a sign from Lucy herself, telling them I was the right animal communicator to work with.

I communicated with Lucy, who came over as a very loving and loyal personality. She described her illness and talked about recent events in her owners' lives, especially connected to their work lives. Lucy shared some images with me: I could see in my mind's eye her owner placing Lucy's ashes on her lap. Validation of the messages I receive from pets who have passed really helps owners build a stronger connection to their pet in spirit. It also helps to remove any feelings of doubt.

When I spotted Lesley and Gill standing on the riverbank during a boat trip I was taking, I had just been thinking that I must be near to where they lived. When we met up afterwards, I was not surprised to hear that it was the very spot where Lucy had taken her last walk. Was it a coincidence? Or guided by Lucy? I had felt Lucy connecting with me in that moment, and I knew she had brought us all together again.

Remember, animals come into our lives for many different reasons. All have a lesson to share and all are meant to cross our path – even if it is for a short time. If we stay open-minded and learn how to communicate with them, we will soon see that our animals have so much to teach us; from patience and forgiveness to compassion and unconditional love.

Using a Medium: How to Avoid the Fraudsters

I feel I should point out that there will always be people who claim to be mediums but who cannot be trusted. They will prey on vulnerable people and often ask for large sums of money for a reading. This is how to spot them.

- They often participate in something called "cold reading". This is when the so-called psychic or medium uses generalized terms that can apply to most people. They may say things like, "I see you've been through a hard time lately," or, "Life has been unkind to you."
- They may tell each person very similar things. The reading will not contain validating specific facts or details that the recipient can verify.
- They may make very vague statements, then take their lead from the client's reaction and encourage them to fill in the details.
- They don't make their charges and the extent of their services clear before you start.
- They can ask for more money than originally quoted for "extra" information or try to scare the client by saying that they have been cursed and will need to pay to have the curses removed.
- They do not offer client testimonials.

Anyone who cannot be verified should be avoided. Here are some tips on finding a reputable practitioner.

- Ask people you trust for personal recommendations.
- Do an internet search for the medium, psychic, therapist or animal communicator that you are hoping to have a reading from and read all the reviews left by others.
- When making your booking, do not be afraid to ask about cost, duration and what to expect during your reading.
- A reputable psychic will always stick to the price agreed.
- Go with your gut feelings: does the medium feel like the right one for you?
- Be prepared to wait. A good medium, psychic or animal communicator will often have a waiting list for readings.
- A good psychic will be happy just to know your first name and will not expect you to give them your full name. You can treat this as confirmation that they work authentically because someone who was planning to do an internet or social media search on you will need your full name to find any useful prior information about you.
- When you find the right animal communicator, relax and enjoy the experience and make sure you record the session or take plenty of notes.

As for your own mediumship skills, we'll look at how you can develop those in chapter 15, when we will explore communicating with a passed pet. Now, let's jump into the more practical part of the book to start learning *how* to communicate with animals.

6

Questions You May Have

As we embark on new learnings we can sometimes feel, especially at the start, that we have more questions than answers, so don't be surprised if this is the case for you right now. Here are some of the questions I often get asked. Knowing the answers now may help you later on.

Why might people try animal communication?

Most people realize their pets are intelligent, and so they want to have as good a relationship as possible with them. People use animal communication for many reasons, including to get to the root cause of a behavioural or health issue, to understand how their pet is feeling and to learn more about their pet's past. It can be helpful to look at the pet's likes and dislikes and to find out if they require any extra help or assistance that their owner can then provide. Sometimes people have unanswered questions or messages that they wish to communicate to a pet that has passed away.

Are all animals psychic?

Yes. I believe all animals have strong psychic abilities and are very advanced in both psychic and telepathic forms of communication. They use this to communicate with each other, as well as with us.

Do all pets go to heaven?

After communicating with hundreds of animals that have passed away, I believe they do reside in the spirit world in the same way that our loved ones pass on but don't cease to "exist". I believe we will all meet again and continue our journey together.

Can you communicate with any kind of animal?

Yes. You can establish a mind-to-mind telepathic contact with any animal who has given their consent and made a pact to speak with you, but what you will learn from the interaction will be unique to that animal. All the case studies I share throughout this book illustrate this point. These stories are inspiring in their own right but also demonstrate just how individual animals are.

Can an animal communicator solve my pet's behavioural issues?

Pets can have behavioural issues for many different reasons. They can stem from a past incident or trauma, incorrect handling or training, abuse or neglect, or for medical reasons. Your pet may even be reacting to something that is happening in your life, and they are picking this up from telepathy or even a change in your demenour. An animal communicator can never promise a resolution to the problem but can often get to the root cause of the issue and shed light on it. See chapter 13 for more on this.

Can an animal communicator tell me if it is the right time to have my pet euthanized?

An animal communicator can offer support and understanding when you are facing a difficult decision regarding your pet. They will not advise you on what to do; that is your decision to make. It is always best to take veterinary advice and to trust your own intuition – you will know when the time is right.

Can I still learn to communicate with animals even though I do not own any pets?

Yes. You do not need to have pets to communicate with animals. All you need is a willingness to learn and an open mind – and, of course, a genuine love for animals. There will be plenty of opportunities for you to connect with people who will allow you to practise communicating with their pets and you can even communicate with wildlife.

Can an animal communicator always find lost animals?

No. Lost animal work is particularly challenging and highly emotional. No reputable animal communicator will ever promise to be able to locate a missing pet. Due to its complexity, not every animal communicator will offer this service. See chapter 14 for more on this.

Can I become an animal communicator as a career?

It is possible to make a career from using your skills as an animal communicator and pet psychic. It can take many months and even years of practice and dedication to become accomplished in this skill. Some people develop more quickly than others. Make sure you practise on a variety of animals and, ideally, participate in an animal communication training workshop with an established teacher. See chapter 16 for more on this.

PART 2

How to Communicate with Animals

Now that we have established the different methods of communication, I am going to teach you how to become a pet psychic and develop the intuitive skills that will help you to better talk to – and listen to – both your own pets and other animals.

This is the practical "How To" part of the book, so it's important not to rush through this section. You will need to read and then practise the exercises I will share with you multiple times. If you don't get the hang of them at first, don't worry. Keep practising, and eventually these skills will become second nature to you.

7

Your Pet Psychic Toolkit

In this chapter we will examine the techniques you will need when communicating with your pet. The elements we will work on include opening your mind, meditation, invisible energy bodies, grounding, and opening and closing down exercises. Think of this chapter as being your pet psychic toolkit.

Opening Your Mind

If you are going to practise any kind of animal communication, it is important that you are in the right frame of mind — relaxed, reflective and open to spiritual and intuitive influences. As the Dalai Lama once said, "The mind is like a parachute; it works best when open."

So let's look at a number of ways you can achieve an open mind.

Relaxation and Achieving Theta State

Feeling calm and relaxed will help you to become aware of the messages that will start to flow into your mind and body. It will also mean you can send your thoughts back to the animal you are communicating with.

Our brains operate at different levels depending on what we are doing. Our brains contain billions of neurons that communicate and connect with each other through small electrical currents. Electrical activity emanating from the brain is displayed in the form of brainwaves. There are four brainwave states ranging from the most active to the least active. When commencing on any kind of telepathic communication and/or psychic development, it is useful to have a basic understanding of these brainwave states and how they relate to accessing an intuitive state of mind.

- Beta is our normal waking state. In this state we are able to make decisions, go about our daily tasks, problem-solve and process information about the world around us.
- Delta is the sleep state. Our body is able to heal and rejuvenate itself and also to enter a dream state.
- Alpha can be described as a "resting" state – you may reach this state if you are taking a break, reflecting, having a rest. It is a very relaxed state of mind that leads into the more meditative theta state.
- Theta state is the state you are looking to achieve before a communication.

Theta State

When you are in theta state, the right-brain hemisphere – associated with creativity and intuition – becomes more active than the left brain, which is associated with logic. Examples of being in a theta state include daydreaming or feeling calmer and more relaxed while doing a creative activity such as painting. It reflects the state between wakefulness and sleep.

The theta brainwave pattern reduces your stress levels, improves your intuition and helps you make a telepathic and psychic connection to the animal you wish to connect with.

When communicating with animals, we are looking to achieve a theta brainwave state. We can access the theta state through deep relaxation and calm meditation. By incorporating meditation practices into your daily routine, you can enhance and strengthen your ability to "tune in" to animal thoughts.

Tips to Help You Relax

Some people find it easy to relax; others don't. Everyone has their own way of achieving relaxation, and no one method is necessarily better than another. You may prefer to focus on music in order to relax, or you may prefer silence. If you are someone who finds it difficult to switch off, here are a few small changes that can help.

- Reduce your caffeine intake. Caffeine is a stimulant and unhelpful when trying to relax. It's far easier to get into a state of relaxation when all stimulants are avoided.
- Try meditation. It calms the mind and will help you to achieve a theta state, making it a useful preparatory technique before embarking on the animal communication session. Deep breathing will help you to focus on the task ahead and will clear away negative patterns of thinking.
- Listen to peaceful music to relax the body and mind, and to create a serene environment.

- Go for a walk. This is a great stress reliever and can allow you to organize your thoughts, especially if you are someone who prefers active relaxation.
- Light a candle to set the mood and create a calming environment. This is a very gentle way to help you relax and will also promote creative thought.
- Burn pure essential oils, such as calming lavender, to help soothe the senses and to create a peaceful atmosphere in which to work psychically.

Achieving a more relaxed state will mean you are more receptive to the messages your pet may be sending you.

Meditation

Meditation has many benefits, including working to relax the mind and release negative thoughts. Relaxation and meditation go hand-in-hand; in fact, they are a bit of a "chicken-and-egg" pairing. Relaxation helps you achieve a theta state so you can meditate; meditation helps you relax enough to get into that state.

During this practice, as the mind becomes calm and focused, we also become more receptive to new thoughts and ideas. And although you are looking to achieve a state of relaxation, you also need to retain a level of alertness and an awareness of what you are thinking.

Meditation is an excellent starting place when learning how to communicate with animals as it will help you focus and apply your mind to the task. Meditation forms the basis for many of the techniques I teach in this book.

When you meditate, you are awake yet aiming for an inner state of peace in which you will not be distracted by external sources. This is a bit like daydreaming, where you allow your mind to wander, and is usually done with your eyes closed.

Most psychics, mediums, clairvoyants, animal communicators and pet psychics meditate regularly because it helps develop our psychic muscle and increases our awareness and intuition.

Meditation can be hugely beneficial for your mind, body and spirit. It allows you to have some time and space to yourself and so can be used for stress relief, as well as to enhance your telepathic and psychic skills.

There are no set rules as to how often you should meditate or how long each meditation should last, but work toward incorporating meditation into your daily routine for around 20 minutes a session in order to reap the benefits.

An Activation Meditation

You will need to meditate and "tune in" to your own energy and psychic powers at the start of any animal communication session or reading, so here is a type of meditation you might like to try. It may be that, as you become more experienced at "tuning in" and getting into a deeply relaxed state ready for psychic communication, you will need less time for meditation and may even be able to drop into the theta brainwave state at will. But, at the start, don't be tempted to cut it short.

Start any meditation in a safe place, away from distractions, and make yourself comfortable.

- Allow your body to feel relaxed and take three deep breaths, breathing slowly and evenly. Close your eyes.
- Imagine in your mind that you are in a beautiful meadow. You can see many different-coloured flowers in the meadow. Imagine you are barefoot and dressed in free-flowing clothing. As you walk through the meadow, the sun is shining, and you can feel its heat on the back of your head. You feel peaceful and calm as you look up at a glorious blue sky.
- Visualize a building in the distance. It looks very old, as if it has been there for hundreds of years. You make your way to the building and approach the front door. The door is locked, but you put your hand in your pocket and pull out a key. The key fits the door lock perfectly, and the door swings open.
- You walk through the door, into a hallway and then on into a large room. Look around this room and pay attention to what you see. Over to the right-hand side, you notice a large bookshelf, so you make your way over, curious to see what it contains. The shelves are full of old and dusty-looking books.
- You are instinctively attracted to a large book on the top shelf. There is a stepladder next to the bookshelf, and you climb the first three steps in order to reach the book that has caught your eye. You pull out the book and blow off the dust and see that it has a blue leather cover with gold

writing on the front. You intuitively know that this book is the key to your understanding of the psychic link between people and animals. As you hold the book in your hands, it feels familiar – as if you have read it before and it has just been waiting for you to rediscover it.

- Imagine yourself now opening the book at the first page. There are three words written there. What do they say? This is an important message for you and one that will assist with your progress as an animal communicator. The words may also be different each time you practise this meditation because you will be at a different stage in your learning and understanding.
- You put this precious book under your arm and make your way back through the room, into the hallway and out through the door. The door closes behind you, but you wisely keep the key in your pocket for the next time you wish to visit.
- As you make your way back through the meadow, the sun is still shining, and the sky is still a deep cobalt blue.

I want you now to count down slowly from five to one. You will then become aware of your current surroundings, and it's time to open your eyes.

Invisible Energy Bodies: Auras and Chakras

An aura is an energy field which surrounds the physical body. It is invisible to our everyday senses, although some sensitive people are able to see different colours in another being's aura.

Animals, just like humans, have an invisible energy body – a unique electromagnetic shield that surrounds the body. In fact, every living thing – including plants – has an aura that is unique to them. Chakras link the layers of the aura to the physical body.

Here, we'll begin to understand how our energy body works and how we can make sure our own life force energy is open, strong and flowing – which in turn will make us more intuitive and sensitive to what's going on with other living things.

Once we have mastered this, we can, if we choose, translate this deeper knowledge of working with energy into a more advanced animal communication and hands-on healing practice, in which we pick up on non-verbal clues from an animal's aura (which we may be able to see) and chakras (which we will be able to "feel" are balanced or not). More on this later.

Auras

You can get a sense of just how powerful your aura is by rubbing your hands together for a couple of minutes and then holding them, palms facing, just a few centimetres apart. What do you feel and notice? There will be heat and a strong feeling of vibration in the space between your palms. This is your own electromagnetic field. Yogis and others who work with their energy bodies (often using the breath and prescribed postures) believe that our auras reach at least 2.7m (9ft) out from our physical body. That means, the next time you are sitting closer than 2.7m (9ft) to a person or an animal, your auras are already merging.

We can use our understanding of an animal's aura to look for energy imbalances, which will then tell us something about their health and happiness. This is quite advanced work because it takes time to refine our skills enough to be able to see and read auras, but it is something worthwhile to aim for.

You can start by thinking of the aura as an invisible energy field that is in fact made up of seven distinct layers that radiate out from the skin of the physical body all the way to the edge of that 2.7m (9ft) reach. These invisible layers, which overlap, or merge into each other, are:

- **Etheric body layer**: this is the closest to the physical body, about 8cm (3in) away. It is connected to the base chakra, which is represented by the colour red. (I'll explain more about chakras further on in this chapter.)
- **Emotional layer**: this is connected to the sacral chakra and is represented by the colour orange.
- **Mental layer**: this is connected to the solar plexus chakra and is represented by the colour yellow.
- **Astral layer**: this is connected to the heart chakra and is represented by the colour green.
- **Etheric template layer**: this is connected to the throat chakra and is represented by the colour blue.
- **Celestial body layer**: this is connected to the brow chakra and is represented by the colour indigo
- **Spiritual** or **soul/ketheric body layer**: this is connected to the crown chakra and is represented by the colour purple.

Auras can actually be "seen" by the use of Kirlian photography, named after its inventor, Semyon Kirlian. He was a Russian scientist who, in 1939, accidentally discovered that when an object is placed on a photographic plate connected to a high-voltage source, it produces an image via the connected camera that is surrounded by colours believed to be those of the individual's aura. If you visit a mind, body and spirit fair, this service is often offered with an interpretation of what your own unique aura colours mean.

Chakras

The invisible chakra energy centres are said to link the physical body to the energy body and the aura. We will look at the human chakras because we want to work on these to increase our psychic abilities, but keep in mind that animals have chakra energy centres too. Chakras are connected to the aura layers, so it's important to understand these first.

In the ancient Indian Sanskrit language, in which many of the yogic healing traditions were first written down, the word "*chakra*" means wheel. The idea is that the invisible internal energy body that links our physical body to our aura is made up of a series of these "wheels" which, if in perfect balance, spin in perfect harmony. If you take a yoga class, your teacher will probably ask you to think about your chakras as being like spinning wheels of white lights that send an invisible life-force energy around your body.

In humans, there are seven major chakras which run in a straight line up the centre of the body from the base of the spine to the crown of the head. Each one is represented by a different colour and connected to a specific body part or system, so each chakra has a different function. Your life-force energy flows through the chakras, unless one is blocked, in which case the flow is interrupted. This does not mean you will be unwell or in any danger; it just means the body may be struggling a little more than necessary to keep going. The chakras are energy centres of great spiritual power, which is why we can work on them to enhance our psychic abilities and use these when communicating with our pets.

The seven major chakras are:

- **Base** or **root chakra**: represented by the colour red. It is located at the base of the spine and its function is to ground and bring us into focus. It is connected to power, stability and survival. Physically, it is connected to the adrenal glands. The areas of the body affected by this chakra are bones and teeth, pelvis and spine, feet, legs and kidneys.
- **Sacral chakra**: represented by the colour orange and located just below the navel. It supervises reproduction, so it is involved in conception and birth. It is also linked to creativity. It's connected to the sex organs. The areas of the body affected by this chakra are the reproductive system, lower back, kidneys and lower digestive system.
- **Solar plexus chakra**: represented by the colour yellow. It is located just below the sternum and its function is associated with motivation, emotions and confidence. It is connected to the pancreas. The areas of the body affected by this chakra are the stomach, digestive system, gall bladder, liver and middle back.
- **Heart chakra**: represented by the colour green. It is located in the centre of the chest. Its function is associated with unconditional love and compassion for others. It is

connected to the thymus gland. The areas of the body affected by this chakra are the heart, the circulatory system, the immune system, the upper back, the all-important vagus nerve (which regulates digestion, heart rate and breathing) and the bronchial tubes and lungs.

- **Throat chakra**: represented by the colour blue. It is located in the neck and connected to vocalization and communication. It is connected to the thyroid and parathyroid glands, which produce the hormone that controls your metabolism (including the processes that convert food to energy). The areas of the body affected by this chakra are the neck and throat, ears, nose and mouth.
- **Brow chakra** or **third eye chakra**: represented by the colour indigo. It is located in the space between the eyes and its function is associated with intuition and inner guidance. It is connected to the pineal gland. The areas of the body affected by this chakra are the eyes, brain and nervous system.
- **Crown chakra**: represented by the colour purple. It is located at the top of the head. Its function is associated with connecting to the higher realms and the divine. When we practise healing or making psychic connections, we are within this chakra. It is connected to the pituitary and pineal glands. The area of the body specifically affected by this chakra is the brain, but it also has an effect on the whole of the body.

Later in the book you will learn more about why it is important to learn to read an animal's external aura and internal but invisible chakra energy centres, especially if you are doing a whole body scan (page 118) – but for now, we will tune into our own chakras in order to become a better animal communicator.

A Guided Chakra Meditation

This meditation will teach you to tune in to the power of your own energy body and use this fine-tuning and awareness to improve your animal communication skills. It is designed to encourage relaxation, to open and balance your chakras and to increase your psychic awareness so that you can connect to your pet more fully. You may want to read and record these instructions so that when you try it, you can concentrate fully on relaxing into the practice.

Before starting any meditation, remember you are always in control. If at any point you want to stop, simply bring your awareness slowly back to your physical body by wriggling your toes and stretching your hands out and then open your eyes.

- Set aside the time to meditate when you know you will not be distracted. Shut off any distractions, such as your phone.
- Use a quiet area or room and make it comfortable with cushions. You can lie on the floor, sit in a chair or lie on the bed. You choose. If you prefer, you can even go outside into nature or meditate in a quiet garden.
- You can light a candle and have some relaxing background music playing. Using pure lavender oil can also assist with the relaxation process.

- Sit or lie down in your comfortable place.
- Close your eyes and take in a deep breath to the count of five. Hold the breath to the count of five and then exhale to the count of five. Do this three more times and allow your body to sink into the chair or bed and feel supported there.
- Imagine you can see a beautiful white light coming into your lungs and filling your body with a powerful healing energy. Feel that you are letting go of any stress and anxiety that you have been carrying around with you and give yourself permission to relax your entire body and mind.
- Now picture all of this amazing white-light energy moving up and down your body from the tips of your toes to the top of your head.
- Allow the muscles in your feet and legs to relax, and extend that relaxation around your lower back and hips.
- Focus on the muscles in your fingers, hands and arms. You may feel a slight tingling sensation as you do this. Take in another deep breath and breathe out slowly while focusing on your shoulders, neck and jaw, as these are the areas of the body where we tend to hold onto tension. Allow yourself to consciously focus on relaxing these muscles, allowing your shoulders to drop as tension eases.
- Think about relaxing the muscles in your face and around your eyes.
- Now focus on the base of your spine and imagine a bright red mist swirling around that area of your body. Imagine you are breathing in the red mist, filling your lungs with its positive energy.

- At the same time, visualize a beautiful red flower located at the base of your spine. See it as a tight bud and, as you focus on it, watch it slowly open its petals and bloom. This signifies your base chakra becoming open and rebalanced.
- Next, think about the colour orange. See, in your mind's eye, a beautiful orange mist that swirls around your sacral chakra just below your navel. Visualize yourself breathing in this beautiful orange mist, filling your lungs with its positive energy. Imagine it as a flower, a tight orange bud that starts to unfold and release its petals. This signifies your sacral chakra becoming open and rebalanced.
- Think about the colour yellow, a beautiful, bright, sunny yellow. Imagine it as a yellow mist swelling around your body. Breathe in the yellow mist and allow yourself to feel calm and refreshed. Imagine a bright yellow flower just below your sternum and see it as a tight yellow bud that starts to slowly open, unfolding its petals. This is your solar plexus chakra becoming open and rebalanced.
- Think about the colour green, a deep, rich green that is pure with healing energy. Imagine it now as a green mist around your body. Take in a deep breath and "see" the green mist filling your lungs. Imagine a green flower in the centre of your chest, a tight green bud that starts to open as its petals fill with green light. This is your heart chakra becoming open and rebalanced.
- Your throat chakra is signified by the colour blue. Imagine a blue mist covering your face and neck. See your body surrounded by this beautiful blue mist and take in a

deep breath. Imagine the blue mist filling your lungs and swirling around your neck. Visualize a delicate blue flower nestling in the centre of your neck – a small bud that starts to open slowly, displaying its magnificent blue petals. This is your throat chakra opening and rebalancing.

- Focus now on your third eye chakra. Imagine a gentle indigo mist floating around your head. Breathe in this indigo mist and focus on the space between your eyes. Imagine an indigo flower in the centre of your forehead. It is tightly closed at first but then starts to open, revealing its beauty. This is your brow and third eye chakra becoming open and rebalanced.
- Now it's time to think about your crown chakra, which is located at the top of your head. Do not be surprised if you have some tingling sensations in this area. Visualize a deep purple mist descending down over your face, head and neck. Now breathe in the purple mist, allowing it to fill your lungs. Imagine a purple flower on the top of your head. This flower has large petals and looks majestic and magical. Its petals shine with a glorious purple light. This is your crown chakra becoming open and rebalanced.
- Now think of all of the chakras and their colours, and imagine them spinning very fast in a clockwise direction, filling your body, mind and very soul full of the energy of healing and vitality.

- Count down slowly from five to one, bring your awareness back to your breathing and then to your physical body. When you are ready, open your eyes.

The meditation is now completed. Allow yourself time to readjust to the waking world. Have a drink of water to ground yourself and bring your energy and awareness back into the physical world.

Key Exercises

I am sharing the basics of a good and safe animal psychic practice here, before we get down to the detail of how we train ourselves in this work. Ritual is important when we work on the psychic planes and with other creatures, so we should never just dive into a session or a reading. As you've now learned, we need to meditate to create the right energy to do this work, but even before that, we need to open up our psychic "zone". This is an important ritual because it allows you to be, and stay, in control of what happens in that space.

When you are ready to communicate psychically, you need to prepare by grounding and opening up. You may need to meditate before starting to communicate to ensure you have reached a theta state. You can then commence your telepathic or psychic work, using the PACT technique. When you have finished, you need to close down again.

A SAFE ANIMAL PSYCHIC PRACTICE PROCESS

Your process should include:

- Grounding exercise
- Protection exercise
- Opening up exercise
- Meditation, if needed (try the Activation Meditation on page 49 or the Hidden Image exercise on page 67)
- Telepathic/psychic work using PACT (chapter 9)
- Closing down exercise

Grounding

Grounding is an extremely important activity to do before commencing any animal communication work.

When we are grounded we feel connected to the earth's energy, and we are positive and focused within the mind and body. If we fail to ground ourselves, we are, in effect, leaving ourselves "open" and vulnerable to things outside our control. We need to protect ourselves when we embark on psychic work of any kind, and grounding is an important part of this. Try this simple exercise:

- Close your eyes, and take three deep breaths. Allow yourself to feel a wave of relaxation starting at your head and your shoulders.
- We often hold a lot of tension around the back of the neck. Focus on this area of the body and roll your

shoulders in a circular motion three times. Allow the muscles to relax and allow this feeling to descend down around your chest, torso, arms and lower back.

- Tell yourself that you feel relaxed and that you give yourself permission to relax the whole of your body. Focus on your stomach muscles, hip area and legs. As you do this, your body may feel as though it is becoming heavy. This is a good sign and shows that your body is responding to your thoughts.
- Visualize green grass in front of you. This grass represents the element of earth. Allow your mind to wander and imagine that you are standing barefoot on the cool, damp grass.
- Now imagine your body is tall and strong like a huge oak tree. Imagine the tree roots growing down through your legs and out through the soles of your feet. These roots go deep into the ground, anchoring you into place. You are now calm and prepared.

Protection White Light Exercise

In talking about the importance of grounding yourself before any form of mediation, deep relaxation or psychic work, I mentioned that one of the reasons this is so important is because otherwise you may be leaving yourself open and vulnerable to things outside your control. I am referring to negative influences or thoughts, and even negative "entities", which may show up uninvited.

While you are communicating on a spiritual plane, it is important to protect yourself against anything you have not invited into your workspace. These exercises will help you protect yourself and stay protected.

- **Protection exercise 1**: Breathe in and out, slowly and deeply, three times. Now imagine that you can see a bright white light. As you see the brilliance of this light, visualize it turning into a mist. Imagine walking into this white mist and it completely covering you from head to toe in its powerful protection.
- **Protection exercise 2**: Visualize yourself in a theatre. You are standing in the centre of the stage looking out toward the audience. The light is dim, but as you take a step forward, the spotlight shines down brightly on you, illuminating your whole body. You are completely submerged in the beautiful, white, protective light.

Opening Up Exercises

There are several ways to open up your mind to the animal communication process, and any one of the following exercises will help you do this. Experiment with all three to find the one that you are most comfortable with.

- **Third eye exercise**: Imagine you can see a large eye situated in the centre of your forehead, in the space between your physical eyes. Imagine this eye is closed but starts to slowly open wide. You can also imagine the colour purple in the centre of your forehead at the same time.
- **Umbrella exercise**: Imagine that you have a large umbrella that has a different colour in each panel. In your

mind's eye, open the umbrella and spin it around your head, acknowledging the different colours in each panel.
- **Light switch exercise**: Imagine you are in a dark room. You switch on the light, and the room becomes bright and illuminated.

You may now need to meditate to ensure you are in a theta state, the most conducive to psychic work. You can then follow the animal communication technique laid out in chapter 6, but you must close down afterwards.

Closing Down Exercise

After any type of telepathic or psychic communication, it is important to close down. It's a signal to say the session is over, and it stops you becoming tired and drained by bringing you back into the real world. It's like leaving a room and switching off a light, or leaving home and locking the doors behind you.

If you like, you can use a closing down technique that is opposite to the one you opened up with, so if you opened with the umbrella, then close it down when you finish. It is fun to practise with these different methods; you will soon find the one that suits you best.

Keep a Journal

We are about to start the exciting journey of learning how to become a pet psychic. Since you will be doing lots of specific exercises (and lots of practice) throughout this book, you might want to start a special journal to make notes and record your progress. Alternatively, you can keep a digital journal. Most smartphones have a voice-recording feature, and this too is an excellent way to keep notes about your experiences

Your journal can provide a record of the results of the practice readings that you do, but, just as importantly, it will be a safe space for you to write down your feelings and thoughts, and to comment on your progress, what works for you and what is more of a challenge. This will be an invaluable resources as you go from strength to strength, building your psychic muscle and practising animal communications.

I use a special journal to record words and phrases from the animal during a session, and I've often found that the doodles and drawings I've done – while, say, waiting for the session to start – carry great meaning too. If you find yourself doing similar, take the time to try to decipher what these symbols and drawings may mean as a part of your psychic communication with that animal.

Record Your Dreams

You can also use your journal to record any meaningful dreams you may have. Now that you are becoming more open and aware, is there a psychic message hidden in your dreams? I often dream that I'm talking to animals. When my beautiful African Grey parrot passed away, just minutes before I arrived home, I was devastated. I wished I had been there a few moments earlier to hold him and comfort him during his passing. Then, two months later, I had a beautiful dream. I dreamt I saw him fly past my living room window, and I ran to the front door, opened it and called his name. He flew down and landed on my arm, and I stroked and cuddled him. The dream felt very real and was what we call a visitation dream. You may have had the same when a pet you loved very much has died but comes back at a later stage to spend time with you in your dreams.

I recorded my visitation dream in my journal, and re-reading it not only gave me great peace but also helped me through my grief over the death of my much-loved bird.

EXERCISE

A Hidden Image

This exercise is really good practice for making sure you get into the relaxed and calm theta state of mind and for helping you to quickly access your intuitive brain in order to start communicating with an animal. Before you do this, don't forget to do the grounding, protection and opening up exercises that I outlined earlier in this chapter. And, at the end, close down before going back into your everyday life. (I will keep reminding you of the importance of these actions until they start to become second nature to you at the start and the end of a session.)

Ask a friend or colleague to place a photograph of one of their pets inside an envelope, making sure you cannot see what's inside. Later, we'll have a look at reading from a photograph, but for this exercise we're more interested in the feelings you receive.

Sit quietly and hold the envelope in between your hands. Close your eyes and allow any thoughts and feelings to enter your mind.

Do you get any mental impressions of what type of animal is in the photograph?

Do you get any feelings about what colour or breed they are?

Do you feel that they are male or female?

Open your eyes and write down your impressions.

Now, open the envelope and see if your impressions match in any way with the enclosed photo. Please don't be disheartened if you struggle to get any strong impressions, or if your first attempts aren't accurate. Practice makes perfect! As your psychic abilities develop, you will notice an improvement.

The exercises in this section are crucial for making sure you're safe and confident before, during and after readings. Think of them as the foundations upon which your readings will be built, and make sure you're confident before moving on.

8

Leaning into Your Abilities

In this chapter you'll find exercises to help you build, and then refine, your psychic abilities.

The more you practise, the more your learning and knowledge will continue to grow – and the more you will become aware that there is always so much more to learn.

As your knowledge and abilities steadily develop, you will learn to rebalance the tendency to focus on the rational left side of your brain by encouraging the imaginative right side of your brain. Any meditation and visualization exercises you do will help you to develop your psychic abilities further.

As with the meditation, grounding, protection, opening and closing exercises in the previous chapter, the exercises here can be used both now and in the future. Make a note of which ones work well for you, then you can return to them a later date.

You might want to do a few of these exercises before starting to communicate with your pet – to get a feel of how you experience messages and begin developing your psychic abilities.

Remember to always do the toolkit exercises in chapter 7 before and after each exercise in this chapter. They will soon become second nature and only take a few minutes. If you have prepared properly, it will make you more receptive to telepathic messages as you will be in the right frame of mind.

Practising Your Telepathic Skills

EXERCISE 1

Telepathy Cards

A great way to practise your psychic skills is by making your own set of "telepathy" cards. These are similar to Zener cards, also known as ESP cards. Zener cards are marked with five different symbols, and there 25 cards that make up the deck; this can be used to carry out clairvoyant tests in which the participants predict the order of the cards one by one.

We are going to do something similar using telepathy cards we can make ourselves. Cut out 10 white cards, approximately the same size as traditional playing cards, from good-quality card stock.

Copy the symbols shown below on the cards in black marker pen. Copy two of each design. It is important to make sure the card is thick enough so you cannot see the symbols through it.

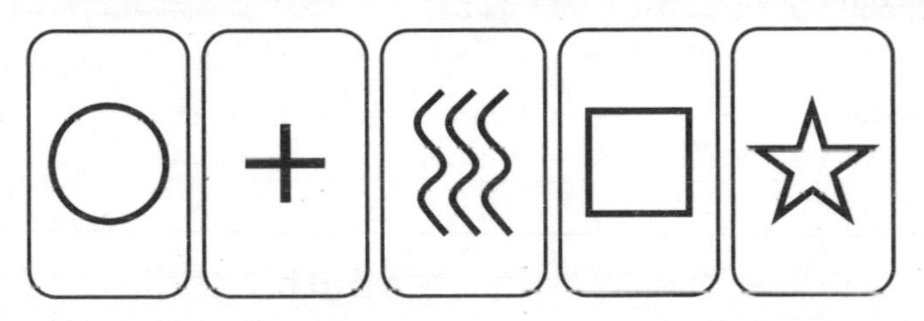

You will now have a set of 10 cards, two of each symbol. Familiarize yourself with the cards and their symbols. You may associate the symbols with something personal to you. For instance, the square may represent a mirror, the star may represent night-time, the circle may represent a clock face, the waves may represent the beach or making waves, and the plus sign may read as positive or an addition of something or someone.

Sit with each symbol and focus on its specific meaning to you.

Now shuffle the cards and place them in a pile face down on the table.

In turn, take a card from the top of the pile and see if you can predict which one will be next.

EXERCISE 2

Sending and Receiving

Once you feel familiar with your cards, you can ask a friend or family member to work with you. Have a set of five cards each, so you both hold one of each symbol.

With telepathy, there is a sender and a receiver. Decide who will be the sender and who will be the receiver.

Allow the other person to look through the cards to become aware of each symbol.

The sender shuffles their cards and, one by one, sends the image on the card through their telepathic thoughts to the receiver. The receiver can either write down the answer or say the answer out loud.

When all five are done then you can swap over.

Stay relaxed throughout.

This exercise takes focus and practice. Do not try to force the thoughts through. Try to clear your mind and imagine that the symbols are appearing on a large TV screen when you receive them.

Keep a score sheet but remember this experiment is more about having the opportunity to practise telepathy rather than the score itself.

Practising Your Psychic Skills

Here are some easy and fun psychic games you can play to expand your psychic awareness.

Playing Card Prediction

Using an ordinary deck of playing cards, shuffle them and then go through the whole pack and predict whether the next card will be black or red.

Repeat the exercise, but this time predict the suit. Then do the same again but predict the number on the card.

Another easy game is to fan the cards out face down and see if you can pull out all the picture cards.

Throwing the Die

Predict which number you will throw. Start with six throws, then expand up to 20 throws. You can take this one step further and make it more complicated for yourself by using two dice.

Who Is on the Phone?

When you hear the phone ring, predict who it is before you look at the caller number display or answer it.

Think about Someone

Focus your thoughts on a family member or friend. In your mind, ask them to call you, text you or send you an email. Set a specific time limit in your mind for this to happen, for example in the next two hours.

Next Colour Car

Observe cars driving past or pulling into a car park. Predict what colour the next car will be. You can expand this further by predicting the make and model of the vehicle.

Who Will Win?

At the start of any TV game show, predict which contestant will win and what the prize will be.

Developing a Deeper Psychic Development

Psychic development will naturally happen alongside your animal communication and pet psychic work. If you would like to focus on your psychic skills further, there is a plenty of information online – but it is always far better to learn from someone who has been recommended by someone you trust.

There is now a variety of spiritualist churches and centres all over the UK, USA and other countries, and these really are great places to meet open-minded people. You can also attend events, which will include psychic development classes and demonstrations of mediumship, meditation and healing.

Psychic Development Circles

These circles are usually held on a weekly basis and run by an experienced spiritualist medium. You might meet at the medium's own home or at a centre. Some development circles are also now available online via Zoom or Skype. They usually run for about eight weeks and can last an hour or two.

The benefits of attending a circle include: connecting with like-minded people; being in a safe place to develop your mediumship and psychic abilities, and deepening your knowledge by participating in exercises to expand your intuition.

Circles are often divided into groups for beginners or advanced students. Development circles may also be offered at your local spiritualist church or centre. See Useful Resources for some starter points.

9

My Psychic Animal Communication Technique (PACT)

In all the previous chapters I've been sharing with you all the important ways we need to prepare ourselves to safely start working as a pet psychic, either with our own animals or with other people's. And now we understand the importance of working in a safe space and using our own energy body to support our psychic abilities (by keeping our aura and chakra energy centres balanced and strong), we are finally ready to start the exciting journey of learning how to be a pet psychic.

The first part of the book was dedicated to all the techniques we can use to really start working our psychic muscle, which may have become flabby through under-use since childhood, but now we have started to reactivate it and harness its power for the greater good of the animals we want to communicate with.

So here we go. Let's get started on the "How to" section of becoming a pet psychic.

I've taught animal communication workshops for many years and, over that time, I have developed my own unique method to help beginners and even students who have had previous experience to quickly attune and access the telepathic and psychic part of their brain. I am convinced, as I said before, that anyone can do this, if they stay open-minded enough to give it a go and believe in their own capabilities.

I call this unique technique my Psychic Animal Communication Technique, or PACT, because, initially, when we plan to communicate with an animal, we are making a pact with them. I can teach you how to make a strong and effective psychic link to an animal, but it will only work providing that both parties agree! We should never *assume* that any animal wishes to communicate in this way; it is always their choice. And so, one of the first things you need to learn is how to telepathically ask for the animal's consent to talk (communicate) together. Making a pact is a mutually beneficial way to help each other and will also help you to build a trusting relationship.

The PACT Technique (Step-by-Step)

I like to teach PACT as a step-by-step progression. Don't be tempted either to rush through the steps or (worse) to skip one. Each step is designed to coach you to the place you need to be in order to communicate psychically with animals. And, of course, as you become more proficient in using PACT, you can start to adapt the steps to suit your own way of working, which may be from photos or in the physical presence of an animal. For beginners, I usually teach PACT *without* the animal being present, but, as you will discover, you can use this same technique if the animal is with you.

Step 1

Do your grounding, protection and opening up exercises from chapter 7. Choose one of the meditation techniques from that chapter to prepare yourself for this work and to trigger the deeply relaxed theta brain state you will need to send and receive telepathic messages to and from an animal. This will feel like a lot to do when you are just starting out, but I promise with practice it will soon feel automatic and perfectly natural to adopt this opening procedure.

Step 2

Once you are "open", take a deep breath in through your nose, hold it for a slow count of seven, then breathe out through your mouth. Do this three times.

Step 3

With your eyes open, take your middle finger and place it on your intuitive third eye invisible energy centre (brow chakra) in the centre of your forehead, between your eyes. Now tap this point with your fingertip gently, seven times. If for any reason you are unable to tap your head, then focus your eyes on a spot on the wall that is just above your head and count to seven. (This will work just as well.)

Step 4

While keeping your finger on your forehead, raise your eyes up as if you are trying to look at your finger but without moving or tilting your head. It will feel as though you are looking up into your eyebrows.

Step 5

Keep your eyes looking upward and slowly close your eyes while keeping the upward stare for approximately ten seconds. This is a safe and effective way to access the theta brainwave state which will facilitate a psychic and telepathic mindset. Now relax your eyes while keeping them closed.

Step 6

Keeping your eyes closed, imagine yourself in a familiar place that you love, such as at the beach, in a field, by a river or even in your own home. See a picture of this place in your mind. It is important that you choose a positive and happy place because this will keep your energy positive and strong, which is what we need when we are about to communicate with an animal.

Step 7

Think of the animal you would like to communicate with. Build a picture of them in your mind by thinking in detail about what they look like.

If the animal is with you, or you have a photograph or a description, open your eyes to look at it for a few moments. In your own voice, within your mind, say their name three times and mentally ask them to join you. (If you don't know their name, just ask them to join you.)

Step 8

You may now have a vision of the animal you would like to communicate with coming toward you. If you are working from a photograph, you may sense their presence and feel as though they are with you. If they are in the same physical space, you may sense them coming physically closer to you. You may even smell them. All this is done within your mind.

Acknowledge how they greet you. Do they seem excited? Do they walk, run, fly or even swim? (Depending, of course, on their species and personality.) Now, mentally ask for their permission to actively communicate with them.

Step 9

Formulate the questions you want to ask, such as, "How are you feeling?" Acknowledge any responses. The answers you receive may seem like your own voice in your mind or may be a vision or thought. You may have a sense of an emotion, a strong gut feeling or even catch the scent of an aroma. Just be observant and stay relaxed during this process.

You may ask other questions but keep them simple. Allow the thoughts to flow between you. Do not try to force anything. You may receive lots of information or just a little. Each animal will respond differently. Try to ask open-ended questions that don't prejudge or influence the answer in any way. The answer may be short or long; just allow the messages to flow without judgement.

Try to stay calm even if you receive emotional messages. You can also ask the animal to tell you more, if you feel it's appropriate.

You can also tell them how much they mean to you.

Finish with a couple of general questions and ask if there is anything you've not asked that the animal would like to tell you about so they can share anything that they wish to offload.

Step 10

Mentally thank the animal for communicating with you.

You may see them leaving your familiar place in your mind's eye, or, if the animal is present in the same physical space, you may feel their energy subtly pulling away from you.

Open your eyes. Record your findings if you wish to do so. Now close down (page 65) to end the session. Once you have closed down, allow yourself a few moments to readjust and absorb what has taken place.

How Does It Feel?

Receiving messages from an animal we are telepathically communicating with is no different to the way we experience the senses in our normal everyday life; we are used to seeing and visualizing pictures in our mind, hearing our own internal voice and feeling emotions and sensations in our body. But what we are aiming to achieve with telepathic or psychic communication is to separate the animal's messages from our own thoughts and feelings. This becomes easier with practice and, as with any new skill, some people will pick this up a little more quickly than others. Don't put pressure on yourself or judge your performance. You will develop at your own rate and in your own unique way.

Just as every animal has their own character and personality, so the way one animal communicates will not be the same as another animal. Some like a short and sweet message, others enjoy going into great detail. Some animals will use more imagery, some will use more words and some will transmit emotions, feelings and even pain. You may, as you learn the techniques to become a pet psychic, find you can taste a particular food in your own mouth, or even that you can smell something. Most likely, you will get a combination of responses, but until you do the reading, you cannot anticipate this. Just accept what comes through, enjoy the process and remember to record it in your preferred way.

Some of my students have told me that when they start to learn animal communication with me, the training wasn't at all what they had anticipated. They expected the process to feel very different from anything they had experienced before – like having a surreal "out-of-body" experience, or hearing a loud stranger's voice talking to them. You will not fall into a hypnotic trance or experience any paranormal type of activity, so there is no need to worry or feel scared before you start. In fact, the whole process will feel natural. You may feel excited, apprehensive, curious or even doubtful about the process before you begin; these feelings are to be expected and are good, as they demonstrate that you care about what you are doing.

Most people describe the experience of communicating telepathically with animals as being as if they are just imagining the messages that are coming through. If that's how it feels for you, then that is exactly how it is supposed feel – as if it's coming from your imagination. This is because you are using the right-hand side of your brain, which is the seat of your imagination. When you receive clairaudient messages, this will most likely sound like your own voice inside your mind. Occasionally it will differ, depending on the animal. This is because your brain understands telepathic language from animals but has to translate the messages into words, pictures, feelings and emotions that make sense to you. When you receive a message, it has been automatically translated into your predominant language. This also means that you really can communicate with animals from any country, and that's why I often describe animal language as a universal one that, with practice, we can all tap into.

Truthfully, the animal communication process itself is relatively simple; the hard part is breaking down the psychological barriers that you will have accumulated throughout your life. Children are often natural animal communicators because they use their imagination all the time, but as we get older we become more conditioned to rely on and look for logical explanations. As children, we are often told that something "is just our imagination", or that we should stop imagining things, so it's no wonder we try to talk ourselves out of telepathic and psychic experiences and allow these doubts to creep in. When you are trying to undo and unravel years of conditioning, you will need to allow yourself time and space to practise. Don't judge yourself or be cross with yourself if things do not go how you had planned or hoped. What is important is that you stay aware of what comes into your mind and pay close attention to your thoughts. Keeping your journal will also help you to see encouraging progress.

It may be that you are already highly intuitive when it comes to animals and their behaviours and preferences, and it may seem that you just "know" why an animal is a certain way. You may feel you are making quick progress through the PACT training, but even so, everyone benefits from practice.

ISABELLE, THE FOX

A few years ago, I visited a wildlife rescue centre run by animal-lover John at his home. It was a privilege to visit, and John, who made me feel very welcome, was open-minded about my pet psychic work. He allowed me to get close to the animals in his care, including several foxes that he had rescued as cubs. I was eager to communicate with a fox and wondered if it would feel different from communicating with a domesticated animal.

I used the PACT technique and initially felt a nervous energy coming from Isabelle, the fox. I knew she'd been with John since a very young age, but I felt she still retained her wild instincts. John offered to take Isabelle out of her pen so I could stroke her if I wanted to; as he approached her, I could sense the close bond between them. I telepathically asked Isabelle what she thought of John. She told me, "I love him." When I told John this, he simply replied, "I love her too."

Isabelle allowed John to take her from the pen and stroke her, as if she was a domesticated dog. I sat on a bench and Isabelle came over and joined me. I telepathically thanked her for allowing me to have this experience with her and asked her if she missed not being able to roam free. She communicated (through words and pictures in my mind) that she was happy and content at the centre with John and all the other animals. This made me feel relieved. After witnessing John and the other volunteers at the centre and seeing for myself how much they are were devoted to the animals in their care, I could understand why Isabelle felt at home there.

If you get an opportunity to visit a wildlife sanctuary, see what information you can pick up from the animals that are being cared for there.

Practise PACT as Much as Possible

To start to develop your pet psychic abilities and PACT, try to put yourself in the path of as many different types of animals as possible. As well as practising with your own animals and those of friends, you can also practise by communicating telepathically with any animal you come across – be that wildlife or in a pet store!

I love to communicate with small pets. I will often wander into a pet store that sells rabbits, hamsters, rats, guineas pigs, mice, gerbils and other small creatures, so that I can have a chat with them to see how they are feeling.

Often the animals are sharing a pen or cage together. Sometimes there are rabbits and guinea pigs in the same enclosure, and they will communicate their likes and dislikes for each other. I often ask them if they are looking forward to getting a new home, if they are well cared for and if they have anything specific they want to share with me.

Once you have mastered some of the basics of PACT, this is something that you might like to try too. Of course, one of the joys of telepathic communication is that no one else is aware of what you are doing!

In the next chapter, we're going to look at how PACT can be used in practice with your own pets.

IDUN AND FREYA, THE SNAKES

Jayne's snake, Idun, was an eight-year-old, 2.5m (8ft) boa constrictor she had owned for just a few weeks. The reading took place via video call, and I could see Idun wrapped around Jayne's shoulders.

Reptiles have always fascinated me; one thing I have often wondered is whether they can feel and even express love for their owners in a similar way to cats and dogs. I was keen to try out PACT on a different kind of animal, and Idun seemed eager to communicate through telepathy. I asked if she could tell me about her past and whether she was happy in her new home with Jayne. Idun (telepathically) answered, "It's like a dream come true. I did not realize that life could offer such bonuses." Then she said, "I can stretch and breathe now."

I asked Idun if she liked to be handled. She replied, "I do not feel threatened here. I enjoy being with Jayne. She handles me safely, as if she's known me for years. I can feel the warmth of her skin and I like it."

I then asked her if there was anything else she would like to share with us. Her reply came in words and phrases into my mind: "Jayne called me cheeky face." Then she showed me an image in my mind of a large camera and said, "I am going to be in a feature film."

When I asked if she needed anything and if she had a message for Jayne, her answers were: "I'm adequately supplied for," and "Jayne's my favourite person; we have a bond."

I thanked Idun for communicating with me and went through my findings with Jayne, all of which she could validate. As soon as she got Idun from her friend, she found her easy to handle, and they had developed a close bond. Idun lives in a large vivarium; she's very observant, watches Jayne and even looks out of the window. Jayne says that holding and stroking Idun is a great way to de-stress.

Jayne laughed when I asked if she had ever called Idun "cheeky face". Jayne had once startled Idun from sleep when she put on the light; Idun had "struck out", and so Jayne called her cheeky. Jayne wasn't aware of any upcoming film roles for Idun but said she would certainly consider them if any opportunities arose. And, of course, she was delighted to know that her snake was very happy.

Toward the end of my session with Jayne and Idun, I became aware of another pet wanting to communicate. This can happen when you open up for animal communication, so don't be surprised if it happens to you. I soon realized there was a second snake – one that Jayne had just rescued – who wanted to tell me her history.

This was Freya, and her messages, which came as strong visions, words and phrases into my mind, told the horrible story of gross neglect that she had suffered before she came to Jayne. I could see her in a small glass vivarium, where she was forced to curl up in an inadequate space. She'd been fed some small mice and chicks that had made her regurgitate and left her feeling listless with no energy. She had been clearly undernourished and told me she had not had enough water to drink and bathe in, which made her feel that her skin was tight, dry and sore. Then Freya gave me a feeling in my own body which I can only explain as an electric shock; at the same time, she told me, "I was zapped and lifted up with a stick." She also communicated that she had been used for breeding and that her babies had been taken away from her as soon as she had given birth; this had made her feel sad. She then showed me a picture of her being put into a bag and taken on a journey in the back of a van.

Jayne confirmed that Freya was in a very sorry state when she was rescued by the police and brought to Jayne to be cared for. All the details Freya had shared were validated. Jayne explained that the electric shock was almost certainly a faulty heat pad – it's common to use a heat pad with snakes, but unfortunately the cheap versions are known to malfunction, resulting in electric shocks or even burns. Fortunately, under Jayne's care, Freya was improving rapidly. Before long, she was placed in a new, safe and loving home.

10

Talking with Your Own Pets

Using the PACT method to talk to your own pets can be really rewarding and is where most people start. However, some find it more difficult to communicate with their own pets because they already have a lot of knowledge and an emotional attachment. Others are concerned that if they communicate with their own pets, they may not like the answers! This is a common scenario, but really it is just a block that we often use to protect ourselves and talk ourselves out of having the experience.

Whether or not you choose to start with your own pet, you'll need to be courageous and to come out of your comfort zone to start a communication session with any animal. Listen to your own instincts and do not push yourself too hard. If you are eager to progress quickly, starting with the option you think is the hardest is often the best place to begin; stay open-minded, throw yourself into the deep end and start with your own pet. (I have mentioned communicating with animals who have crossed over into the spirit world, but when starting out as a pet psychic, it is usually easier to begin with a pet that is still living.)

Starting with your own pet means you don't need to look at a photograph or even be in the same room as your animal because you already know them. Ideally, you will be sitting comfortably in a chair or lying down with your eyes closed. Have a pen and paper close to hand to record your findings at the end of the session. Please be aware that you may find communicating with your own pet a little emotional at times, and you may even shed a tear or two (keep a tissue at the ready). However, it will more likely be a pleasurable and enlightening experience and one that can provide great insight, helping you with your personal healing journey as well as theirs.

Before you start, set and hold the intention that you are going to have a telepathic and psychic link with your pet.

Now, let's get started.

You are going to be using telepathy, which means you will be sending and receiving messages mind-to-mind. It's a two-way process and an exchange of thoughts and energy. Think of it like a radio – the transmitter sends out a frequency and the receiver tunes in to listen.

To begin, I'm going to suggest some questions to ask the pet you are communicating with, but later on, you will be encouraged to think of your own relevant questions. You will be predominantly working in a clairaudient way when asking these questions. In other words, you will say the questions in your mind with the intention of your pet hearing them. You can also use clairvoyance to transmit pictures and visions in the same way.

Holding the intention that the animal you are communicating with can receive the information you are sending is a key factor in successfully creating the link. Not judging or pre-empting information that you receive will assist you greatly. Accept that the thoughts, visions, feelings and emotions that you experience are being transmitted to you from your pet; this will help to convince you that the process is real.

PACT in Practice

Prepare yourself for the reading; follow the steps outlined in the previous chapter in my PACT technique, and invite the animal you want to communicate with to join you in your special place. Say their name once more in your mind and acknowledge how they greet you. For instance, do they run or walk toward you? Ask them to sit or stand beside you. Stay observant; did they bring anything with them? This may be a favourite toy or possession. It's now time to talk to them – from your open mind to theirs.

First, say:

"Thank you for joining me in this way. I am open to communicating with you. Do you agree to communicate with me?"

Acknowledge the answer. It will sound like a thought in your mind or maybe you'll be shown a picture.

Next, ask your pet:

"How are you feeling?"

Be observant of the answer. Did it sound like words in your mind? Maybe you had a strong feeling or emotion or even a mental vision?

The next step is to tell your pet how you feel about them. Mentally send the words you wish to use or even a symbol, such as a love heart or a smiley face. Be observant of the answer they send back into your mind.

A good thing to ask your pet is:

"Can you recall a happy memory that we shared together?"

Stay open to receiving this information through thoughts, words, phrases, pictures and feelings.

Then transmit this question:

"Is there anything I can do to improve your lifestyle or environment?"

Do you get any images, words or phrases coming into your mind about improvements that can be made or anything else that they need?

You can also ask your pet:

"Is there anything you would like us to do together?"

You may see a picture of an activity or something you used to do in the past.

You can choose your own questions too. These could be about your pet's health or behaviour. You may choose to ask about their food and diet; you can check to see if they are happy with the equipment or bedding that you are providing.

If you have a new pet and don't know much about their background you can ask them:

"Can you tell me about your life before we met?"

This can be quite revealing but also very emotional, especially if you have adopted or rescued an animal. Just take things slowly, don't rush and do not anticipate their answer.

You can try this exercise as many times as you like with any of your pets. It gets easier with practice. You can also sit with a pen and paper and draw a cartoon of your pet with a speech bubble coming out of their mouth, with the words inside that you feel they are telling you.

Tell your pet that you are very happy that they communicated their thoughts with you today, and say thank you as a way of ending the session.

Close down by using one of the previously suggested close-down methods in chapter 7. Open your eyes now and write down your findings in your dedicated journal.

This can be a very emotional exercise for an animal lover, and each person will experience something different. Every animal is an individual and may transmit messages in different forms. You may have received a lot of information during this exercise, or you may not have received much. Communicating with our animals requires patience, practice and self-belief, and the more you try it, the easier it becomes.

If you communicate with your pet when you are physically together, you can try stroking them at the same time or looking into their eyes. (It's worth noting here that dogs can take this as a sign of aggression if they don't know you well. If you recently got a rescue dog, for example, build trust before staring into their eyes.) Some pets will react during this process. They may shake their head, look puzzled or look around as if trying to work out what is happening. Sometimes they become excited, and sometimes they will just go to sleep. Your job is to stay calm and focused throughout, which will be reassuring for the animal who has made a pact to communicate with you.

ROSIE AND LILY, THE HORSES

Lauren explains:

I had my first reading with Beth ten years ago when I asked her to communicate with my horse Rosie, who is now 24. I had sent Beth a photo of Rosie in advance of the reading and couldn't wait to hear what Beth would say about her. She is a very sensitive and difficult horse, but I am very connected to her.

In that first reading, I also received messages from my miniature Shetland pony, Raffy, who is now 15. Beth picked up that Raffy is a very cheeky pony and a very different character to Rosie, which is true.

Raffy gave Beth the name "Ben". He told her he found Ben really funny and said that whenever Ben gets a date with a girl, he brings her up to the yard to see Raffy because Raffy is really cute, which makes for a nice first date.

Ben is my brother! When I asked him if what Raffy said was true, he said, "Yes, I take the girls to the yard all the time to see the horses."

More recently I have had readings with my horse Lily, who has been unwell. It really wasn't nice to ride her, and she was always trying to throw me off because she was in so much pain, so I wanted to find out more about what was wrong with her and to know if I could do anything else to help her. During the reading, Lily gave Beth the name "Helen". Beth told me that Lily wanted me to call Helen. The only

Helen I knew was my saddle-fitter. Helen came out to look at my saddle and said there was nothing wrong with it, but she decided to change the bar inside just in case. When she took the bar out, we saw that it had snapped inside and that's what was causing Lily so much pain. I was stunned.

I have learned from Beth how to access my own clairaudience abilities so that now I can listen to my animals too and really understand what they are saying to me. I have started to trust what my gut is telling me, and most of the time, I'm right. I have received many confirmations and validations that what I have picked up when communicating with my animals has been accurate. And I feel strongly that everybody who has pets will benefit from listening to them and being open to their messages.

My response:

I believe Lauren is a natural animal communicator, as she describes being able to hear her horses, and I have encouraged her to trust those messages. This has led to her becoming more interested in psychic subjects and gaining knowledge about animal spirit guides. It gives me great pleasure to see clients blossoming and following their own spiritual pathway, and I do my best to encourage and support them through their development. Lauren proves that if you are open to the concept of communicating with your pets, you too can achieve this skill.

Meditation for Communicating with Horses

This meditation is particularly helpful if you want to communicate with horses but can be adapted for any animal, taking into account their natural environment.

Sit or lie down in a safe and comfortable place and follow your meditation, opening and protection rituals. Following the PACT steps (see chapter 9), begin by taking a slow deep breath in through your nose and out through your mouth. Repeat this three times.

Allow any tension in your muscles to melt away. Focus on one part of your body at a time. Start with your feet and your legs and allow them to feel heavy; think about slowly relaxing each muscle, bit by bit. Now focus on the lower back and your tummy muscles. Allow the tension to drift away and feel the sense of relaxation moving up through your body, around your hands and arms, your chest, shoulders and neck. Focus on relaxing your shoulders and notice how they gently drop down as they become less tense. Allow this relaxation to extend around the base of your neck and around your jawline. Concentrate on the muscles around your eyes relaxing, too.

I want you to imagine that you are in a beautiful meadow. The grass beneath your bare feet is green and cool. The sky is bright blue, and the air is fresh and crisp. You can feel the warm rays from the sun on top of your head extending all the way down your back.

You look around and in the distance you see the most beautiful stallion that you have ever seen. He has a long silky mane and tail, a slender body and strong, muscular legs. You can see his rich colour and you know his name.

You instinctively run up to the horse, and as you approach he neighs as if to say "Hello!" He lowers his head for you to stroke his face, and then you put your arms around his neck and run your hand along his back. As your hand touches the flat of his back, the horse looks round as if inviting you to mount. Imagine that you now jump up onto his back, taking hold of a handful of his mane to steady and balance yourself.

The horse starts to trot and then canter through the meadow. You can smell the sweetness of the grass and feel the breeze blowing through your hair as you glide along. A pathway emerges and the horse follows it. There is no need to guide him, as you are just enjoying the ride. At the end of the pathway is a clearing. You can feel the horse slowing down as he approaches this clearing. Before he reaches a standstill, you slide gracefully off his back, and as you land on the ground he turns and places his head in your hands. You look directly into the horse's eyes and in your mind you hear the horse say, "I have an important message for you." Allow this important message to flow into your mind and acknowledge its meaning.

Now thank the horse for sharing the message, which you instinctively understand the importance of, and imagine yourself walking back into the grassy meadow. You feel safe and enlightened by this experience. Count down slowly from five to one and then open your eyes.

Make sure you record the message as relayed to you by the horse. If at first you don't understand it, go back to your journal when time has elapsed and see if it makes more sense to you now.

PHOEBE, THE BLACK MARE

Ali explains:

My daughter's pony, Phoebe, was a little black mare. We knew that she had previously been rescued and was a sensitive soul. During a reading, Phoebe told Beth that she hated the sound of Velcro – and wasn't that just the truth! We already knew not put anything on her that fastened with Velcro, otherwise she would jump out of her skin. She also asked us to promise never to sell her. This tear-jerking request was a pleasure to honour, despite my daughter, Olivia, having outgrown her.

A few years after, a friend asked if she could borrow Phoebe for their little girl. I knew that Phoebe would have a fantastic (temporary) home on their farm and that the little girl adored her. I thought that this would be a perfect solution and would give little Phoebe a purpose again. But two days before she was meant to leave, Phoebe started acting oddly and was staggering around. The vet admitted her condition was baffling and, despite our further attempts to cure her, Phoebe sadly had to be put to sleep. There is no question in my mind that the little pony really was determined never to leave us.

My response:

When I first communicated with Phoebe, Ali's pony, it was clear to me that she'd had a troublesome past and, as a result, was nervous and sensitive. Ali confirmed that Phoebe had been rescued. Phoebe gave me the sound of ripping Velcro. Then she gave me an image of the rug that she wore in bad weather. I knew the sound of Velcro upset her and asked why. Phoebe told me that it sounded like the noise from a whip and that she had been whipped in the past. The unkindness she had experienced at the hands of a human explained why she was nervous.

Phoebe was giving me happy thoughts about feeling secure in her home with Ali and her family; I distinctly heard the words, "Promise not to sell me," and I passed this message on. It was clear to me that Phoebe had found a wonderful, kind home, and, having developed a trusting bond with Ali and her daughter, Olivia, Phoebe wanted this to be her forever home.

What Phoebe demonstrates so clearly is that animals do not forget their pasts and can carry trauma with them, just like people do. But the good news is that the communication process acts as a way for us to understand what has happened to them and so can have a positive effect on their wellness. It is healing for animals (just like people) to release their thoughts and to share their issues.

Letting Your Pets Help You

I believe that our pets have an innate sixth sense and are able to foresee future events and outcomes for us, and so here is a technique I use regularly with my pets: I ask their opinion about all sorts of topics that go on in my life. You can learn to do the same by practising this exercise. Remember to do your preparation exercises from chapter 7 first.

Think of a specific situation that is currently going on in your life; something that you would like some help and guidance in dealing with. This could be about getting a new job, looking for a new relationship or working out how best to deal with a friend or family member. Maybe you have a difficult decision to make, and you cannot decide what to do for the best, or maybe you are thinking about leaving your job and starting your own business.

On a piece of paper, write down these words:

I would appreciate some guidance about [write down your situation].

Think about the pet that you would like to help you, and write their name on the same piece of paper. Now say your pet's name in your mind three times followed by:

I would appreciate some guidance about my situation.

On the same piece of paper, start to write down anything that comes into your mind: it may be a word, a phrase, someone's name. Just allow the pen to write down your thoughts until you feel you need to stop.

Now, underneath this, write the words:

What could I do next?

Once again, allow the thoughts to come into your mind and write them down. Even if it seems as though what you are hearing or seeing is not making sense, write it down regardless.

Now write down the next question, which is:

What will be the possible outcome?

Allow the thoughts to enter your mind without judgement. Jot everything down until it feels it has come to a natural close.

Now, in your mind, thank your pet by saying:

Thank you for help and insights.

Next, fold up the piece of paper and carry it around on your person for an hour or so. Then, when you feel ready, sit quietly, open up the paper and read what you have written. By now it should start to make sense.

It may help you form a plan of action to deal with the situation. Think about the advice you have received.

- How does it make you feel?
- Did anything surprise you?
- Did you expect the advice that came through to you?
- What do you think about the possible outcome?

You can use this exercise whenever you have an issue or dilemma to resolve.

ELLIE, THE WARMBLOOD MARE

Ali explains:

I owned a gangly, chestnut warmblood mare called Ellie, who was from Germany. She was a diva from the beginning but was very sweet natured and didn't have a nasty bone in her body. It was just that when she wasn't happy, she made sure that everyone around her knew about it. I called on Beth's animal communication expertise to help us manage Ellie's strong personality.

It was clear from the reading that I had purchased an equine version of a high-society diva and snob with an opinion on everything. Beth said that Ellie spoke to her with a very posh voice and thought that her breed brand (which warmblood horses have on their flanks) was unsightly! She admitted to Beth that she was highly strung and bragged that she liked to assert herself in the herd (she was *always* the herd leader), and that she found the other horses to be irritating and common. She felt herself to be very clever (that was true), but she could also be demanding. She wanted her feed bowl washed out after each meal; she said we needed to add hot water to her water bucket to take the chill off in winter, and she was always quick to let us know if her saddle needed adjusting!

But Ellie was also very wise and would often give me advice, communicating through Beth to tell me not to worry and to calm down. She even advised me to change my diet and wasn't shy about coming forward with her opinions of my ex-husband while we were going through our divorce.

Sometimes Ellie would come out with what seemed like random comments during her readings, some of which would not make sense at the time. Flicking through my notes, I recently came across one of these random statements from about six years ago: "Someone has dislocated or is going to dislocate a knee."

It wasn't until that moment that I realized this prediction by Ellie was about my son. He dislocated a knee about a year after this reading and went on to dislocate it twice more. As I write this, these dislocations are causing problems with his application to join the RAF. I now understand that Ellie knew this would happen; however insignificant that statement seemed at the time, it is so significant now.

Sadly, I recently lost Ellie, but no doubt she will start coming through from the spirit world in my future readings with Beth.

My response:

It was clear that Ellie liked things to be done her way, and, although kind and sweet-natured, she was also bossy and assertive. Ellie was more than happy to share her opinions, likes and dislikes. I will never forget her showing me a picture in my mind of a kettle boiling. I could then see the hot water being poured into her water bowl. Clearly,

Ellie did not like to drink cold water, preferring it to be warm. Ali confirmed that this was true.

Ellie communicated to me in a very honest way. She recalled past events by showing me pictures in my mind of what had taken place, repeating words and phrases that she had heard from people talking. I wrote everything down so as not to forget anything. Ali then validated these messages, which gave proof to the process. Ellie was often highly entertaining to communicate with; I never knew what to expect from her and that reminded me to stay non-judgemental when doing this work.

11

Telepathic Communication Using a Photograph

We've learned now how telepathic and psychic communication with animals can be done at a distance, so you don't need to be physically present with the animal in order to have a successful communication. This has the advantage that the animal can be anywhere in the world, and also that you can be in your own home and do the reading when you feel it is most appropriate.

It's always helpful to know the animal's name, as this can make things easier when reporting back your findings. Then, all you need is a clear photograph, print or digital, although some people report finding it easier to link with the animal when holding a physical photograph in their hand. You don't have to use just one photograph either. For the best readings, it is ideal to have a close-up shot of the animal's face, so that you can look into the eyes, then full-body shots from each side and from the back. This will allow you to focus on any areas of the body which may be out of balance. (We will later explore some body scanning techniques in which a clear full-body image will be used.)

Some people actually find it easier to use a photograph to do a reading rather than in person because you are not distracted by the animal or looking for physical responses or cues while you are making your link with them. And if you are communicating with your own pet, it can help to keep some emotional distance between you, which will also help prevent any mental blocks.

Don't forget to have a pen and paper or your journal handy to write down the information you receive or, if you prefer, record it on your phone.

Try Reading from a Photograph

It doesn't matter that the animal you are going to link with is not physically present; it is still important to meditate to switch your brain to the calming and receptive theta brainwaves, and don't forget to do your grounding, protection and opening up exercises, as well as closing down when your session has finished.

Once you have a photograph of the animal you plan to communicate with, go back to my instructions for the PACT technique and work through each step until Step 7. Then open your eyes and look at the photograph in your hands. (You can then, if you prefer, close your eyes again while communicating.)

Mentally introduce yourself to the animal and ask for their permission for the communication to take place. Sit quietly and start to absorb any initial impressions that you get, such as, "This dog looks friendly," or, "That cat looks unhappy," and so on.

You may start to receive information immediately, even before you have formulated any questions, as your body picks up thoughts and feelings from the pet. If so, note these down in your journal. This should all feel very natural and not at all strange or scary.

It's easy to miss subtle changes in the way you feel, so try to pick up on each thought and feeling that comes to you, no matter how insignificant it may seem. Now acknowledge if you feel any different from before you looked at the photograph. If so, note it down and start to formulate and ask questions in your mind. You may have some pre-prepared questions that you wish to use. Focus entirely on the animal and trust in yourself.

Let's start by telepathically asking this simple question:

How do you feel?

Repeat this question in your mind as you look at the photo, focusing on the animal's face and eyes. If you know the animal's name, then say it in your mind three times, just as you did when practising with your own pet.

Now acknowledge the answer that you receive back from them. It normally comes quickly and can come in various forms. First, notice if you feel any particular emotion – such as happy, sad, excited, calm, anxious, agitated, scared, nervous, frustrated, angry, confident.

Do you feel any physical sensations in your body? This can include feelings of tiredness, alertness, and of feeling well or out of balance. This can often feel like a quick twinge in your body that only lasts for a couple of seconds. A twinge in the back, for instance, may indicate discomfort in that area of the animal's body. Each part of your body will correspond with theirs; where their body differs from yours – such as having a tail or wing – they will communicate this through another one of your senses.

Check in with yourself by asking the following questions:

- *Are you receiving any internal dialogue in the form of words and phrases in your mind?*
- *Are you receiving any images, pictures or thoughts?*
- *Are you receiving any smells or tastes?*

Make a note of everything that comes to you. Even if something does not make sense at the time, it's still important to keep a record of it.

Now move on to your next question and use the same process, breaking each part down and making a note of it.

As you progress, you may find that one or two of your senses seem stronger than the others. This will be a reflection of your own personality. If you are more of a talker, you will most likely receive lots of words. If you are more of a visual person, you are more likely to receive pictures and images. If you are a compassionate person, you may receive lots of feelings and emotions, and so forth.

It also depends on the personality of the animal. Just like people, some animals are chattier and more enthusiastic than others. Some animals may be naturally shy or just be so content with their lives that they don't necessarily have as much to divulge. The more animals that you can communicate with, the more you will experience these differences.

Useful questions to ask include:

- Can you describe your personality?
- What do you like to do?
- Can you share a memory with me?
- Is there anything that you need right now?
- Is there anything you would like your owner to know?
- Do you have any experiences you wish to share with me?
- Is there anything else you would like to tell me?

Observe what messages come to you using the same process.

You can think of your own questions and, of course, experiment with both simple ones and others that give an opportunity for more detailed answers. If you do not get an answer, then move on to your next question. You can also communicate without any questions by just saying, "Let's talk" or "I'm listening".

RELAYING YOUR FINDINGS

If you are reading a photograph for someone else, be mindful of how you deliver any sensitive messages to the animal's owners.

Some messages may be emotional and upsetting, especially in the case of rescued, neglected or otherwise abused animals who may divulge upsetting details about their past. You might want to refrain from going into graphic detail while still delivering your findings in a compassionate way.

If you receive messages about the animal's health, then remember to suggest that the owner passes that information on to a qualified vet, especially if the health condition is a serious one that clearly needs professional treatment.

Remember, too, to keep the message pure and not try to make sense of it or interpret it yourself.

Exercises to Practise Reading from a Photograph

What follows here are three animal profile exercises, so you can try reading from a photograph. You may find these difficult at first, so don't feel like you have to do all three exercises at once. Try one, check your results at the back of the book, take a break and recharge, then come back and tackle the next one. Remember, you're at the start of your journey; don't worry if you struggle.

ANIMAL PROFILE EXERCISE 1

Monty

Here is a photo of Monty. He is seven years old. He was rescued with his sister Minnie when they were two days old.

In this photo you can clearly see Monty's eyes.

I am going to suggest some questions to ask Monty. These questions will be similar to the questions you can ask your own pets, so it's a good way to practise sending and receiving information and getting into the flow of telepathic communication.

Use the PACT method and, at Step 7, open your eyes and gaze into Monty's eyes in the photo. (This is something you can try with your own pets, too.) While looking into his eyes, ask his permission for the communication to start.

Now let's ask Monty the following questions:

- What do you enjoy doing?
- What food do you like to eat?

- Is there anything that you need to improve your lifestyle?
- Can you tell me about your health?
- Can you share a happy memory with me?

Now thank Monty for helping you practise your communications skills, and close down.

Record the information that you picked up.

Turn to page 221 to find out whether you came close to the truth about Monty.

ANIMAL PROFILE EXERCISE 2

Claude

Here is a photograph of Claude, a beautiful white cat with black markings and a black tail.

Follow the PACT to link with Claude. At Step 7, look directly into his eyes in the photograph. Speak from your mind to Claude's and ask the following questions:

- Can you tell me anything about your history and background?
- What are your likes and dislikes?
- Do you have any health issues?
- Do you have a favourite toy?
- What do you enjoy doing?

Thank Claude for communicating with you, use a closing down exercise and note down your answers.

When you have finished, turn to page 222 and find out how accurately you answered the questions.

ANIMAL PROFILE EXERCISE 3

Get to Know Three Dogs

Look at the photograph overleaf of three female dogs. From left to right, their names and breeds are Misty, a white Chinese Crested Powder Puff; Tilly, a white and tan Jack Chi; and Vivienne, a fawn Jack Chi. Misty and Tilly live together, and Vivienne visits and stays with them while her owner is on holiday.

Follow the established PACT to communicate with each dog individually.

- Which dog do you feel is the most dominant?
- Which dog used to live in Poland?
- Which dog has had her front teeth removed?
- Which two dogs have had their names changed?
- Which dog is the oldest?
- Which dog is the youngest?
- Which dog had an ingrown claw?
- Which one was previously used for breeding purposes?
- Which one used to be called "Princess"?
- Which dog barks at the vacuum cleaner?
- Which dog is frightened by newspapers?
- Which dog refuses to eat rice?

- Which dog has previously suffered from gastroenteritis?
- Which dog participates in dog yoga?
- Which dog wears a red coat?
- Which dog regularly travels by train?

Try not to over-think your answers. Go with the first thoughts that come into your mind. Do not put pressure on yourself if you are struggling to receive an answer; move on to the next question. Animal communication should flow effortlessly and quickly.

Record your answers in your journal and turn to page 223 to find out about the three dogs.

Conducting a Body Scan

Another way to communicate through a full-body photograph is to do a whole body scan. This is a useful way to check over the animal's body to identify areas that are out of balance and may be causing either health or behavioural problems or both. The purpose of this is not to diagnose an illness, but it can elicit useful information that the owner can then share with a vet or other health professional.

As usual, follow my PACT steps as outlined in chapter 8.

Take your time to look at each section of the body, starting from the head. Allow your eyes to scan over the picture(s).

What areas of the body do your eyes feel drawn to?

Now take your index finger and run it over the photo in the same way, starting from the head and covering each area of the body.

Does your finger naturally stop at a certain area or point on the body? (Sometimes it feels as though your finger is stuck on a certain area.)

You will remember that in chapter 6 we looked in detail at how we could tune into our own invisible chakra energy centres to improve our psychic awareness and learn more information during a reading. And I told you animals have auras and chakras too and that it's possible to include these energy readings in a body scan. This is quite advanced work – but give it a go!

You can incorporate the chakra system into the body scan by following the method below.

Imagine the seven major chakras represented by their corresponding colours in the relevant part of the animal's body. (Go back to chapter 4 to remind yourself of each of the chakra energy centres.)

Which colours are the brightest in your mind? This indicates wellness and balance.

Which colours look dull? This can indicate an imbalance in that area.

Now turn to your own body: does any part of your body feel out of balance? Do you have any unusual sensations? This can also be an indication of an area of the animal's body that is out of balance or may need further assistance or treatment.

Record your findings.

ANIMAL PROFILE EXERCISE 4

Fred

Fred is a chestnut-coloured horse and is 16 hands high. Let's do an animal communication reading of Fred using a photograph, followed by a body scan, as described above.

Prepare and use the PACT and the communication techniques we have learnt so far.

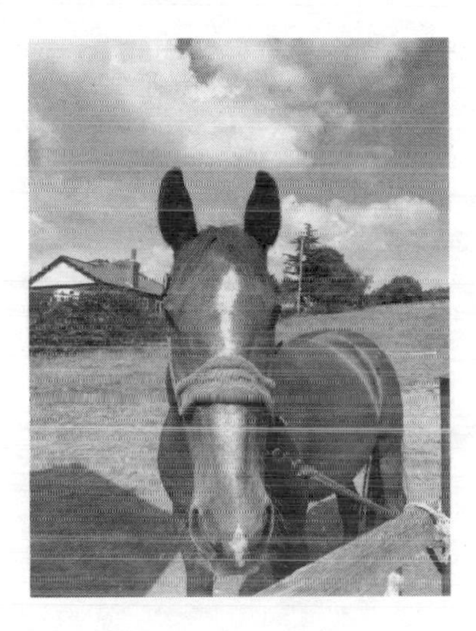

When you have prepared yourself in the usual way, telepathically ask Fred the following questions.

- How old are you?
- Can you describe your personality?

- What do you enjoy doing?
- What is your background?
- What have you done in the past?
- Do you have any animal companions?
- Do you have any advice for me?

Thank Fred for communicating with you.

Now let's perform a body scan on Fred using the pictures here, and the techniques I have already described (page 117).

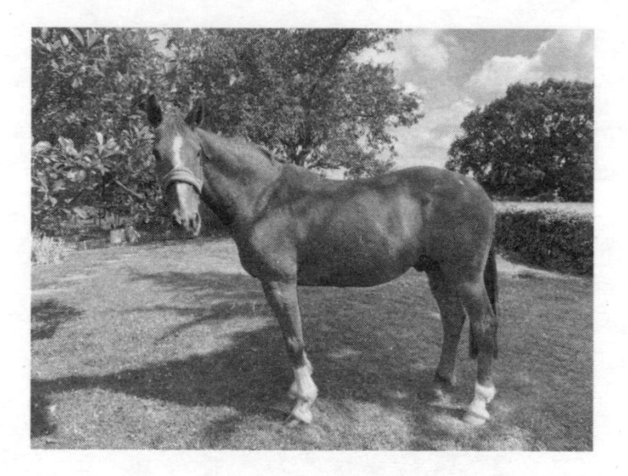

Remember that with a body scan we are also going to tune into the animal's invisible energy centres – or chakras – to see what information they reveal as we scan our eyes and trace our fingers over Fred's whole body. Do not rush this exercise. The more you can focus, the more information you will receive to help answer your questions.

Jot down your findings, then see how much you can validate from the information about Fred on page 225.

12

Communicating with Other People's Pets

Communicating with other people's pets is an excellent way to put your skills to the test because you can ask for feedback (and thus validation) from the pet's owner. This can really help to quash those normal but undermining feelings of self-doubt that inevitably creep in when we are first learning to trust our intuition. Remember not to allow the fear of getting something wrong to hold you back. Get into the habit of writing things down without analysis; keep it pure. You may not understand a message yourself, but the owner will recognize it – if not now, then at some point in the future when they go back to it (as we have seen from some of the case histories I have shared).

The process when you read for someone else's pet is exactly the same as for all the readings we have done so far; you can read with the animal present or use a photo or a description from the owner to open up and start the conversation.

I was teaching a workshop a few years ago when two of my students (who had both brought photographs of their pets with them) paired up together to practise on each other's pets, a dog and a horse. The dog had sadly passed away, and the horse was still very much living. The two women swapped photos and sat quietly to practise a communication. I encouraged them to write down everything they received and to take turns to share their findings and messages. The lady who was communicating with the dog said, "I am really struggling, I'm so sorry. All I have written down is 'green frog'. I don't think I've done very well, and I don't know what it means, but I could just see a green frog in my mind."

At this point the other lady burst into tears. "That's amazing," she said. "A green frog was my dog's favourite toy. In fact, he loved it so much that we buried him with it."

I wanted to share this story to stress the importance of keeping a message pure and of having the courage to share what you experience and telepathically receive with your client. And, of course, when you get positive confirmation (validation) about the messages you pass on, it will boost your growing confidence and encourage you to keep practising.

Your Reading

Think about breaking down your reading into distinct sub-parts to include the following:

- A description of the animal's character and personality.
- An examination of any health concerns (remembering to advise your client to seek a professional vet's opinion if they have medical concerns).
- An exploration of any behavioural issues.

- Any information about the animal's past.
- Information about the animal's present circumstances, how they are feeling and any potential improvements they have asked for.
- Any additional messages for the client from the animal.
- Any additional questions the client wishes to pose.

What to Expect from the Animal

Every reading will be unique, but these are some common elements that often arise:

- How they feel, physically, mentally, emotionally and spiritually.
- Information about their past, present and even what the future has in store for them.
- Their likes and dislikes.
- Their current lifestyle.
- How they are behaving and why.
- Significant people's names.
- What their life purpose is.
- Advice and messages for their owners.
- Advice and messages for you!

Validation of Your Work

It is hugely rewarding to have your readings validated by the owner or by someone who knows the animal well. It's an even bigger confidence boost to have your work validated by a professional, such as a vet, animal behaviourist, chiropractor or other qualified professional. The more validations you gain, the less self-doubt you will have. Remember, we are human and we are all capable of making mistakes. If you make a mistake, don't get hung up on it, just acknowledge it and move on.

A FRIEND'S DOGS

Smita explains:

I am an energy healer but am new to animal communication. I am open-minded and have an interest in spiritual topics, but I wasn't sure PACT would work for me. Beth reassured me that it would, as long as I had an appreciation of the animal kingdom, which I do.

I contacted a friend who sent me some photographs of his two dogs for me to practise with. I had never met the dogs and did not know any specific details about them.

I began by doing some deep breathing exercises. I then grounded and protected myself and opened up. I followed Beth's PACT instructions, and when I got to Step 7, I looked at the dog pictures and focused on just one of the dogs, a white poodle. Immediately, I saw a picture in my mind of this dog shaking inside a cardboard box and sitting on a little pink blanket. I also had a picture of her stretching her legs out after going for a walk.

I asked the dog about her background, and she showed me that when she had been separated from the rest of the litter, she had felt scared, alone and unloved. Then she was taken to a place with lots of other dogs, which she didn't like as there was too much going on. Even with the other dogs around, she still felt alone. I felt that she was quite snappy and would warn other dogs to keep away from her.

Then I asked her if she was happy in her current home. Instantly, I felt her mood change, as if she was getting excited, and I had a feeling of happiness from her. She wanted to thank her owners for loving her and taking her in.

At times during the reading, I felt as though I could hear a voice inside my head as well as seeing visions and experiencing strong feelings. But, at first, it did also feel a bit like I was making it up or imagining it.

I moved on to the next photo, which was of a Jack Russell. I felt that this dog was quite active. I asked her, "How are you today?" and had a vision of her going backward and forward from the garden into the house as if she was checking on someone. I got the impression that she would keep herself busy doing that. Then I could see her having a snooze.

I asked her, "What happened to you in the past?" She showed me a white van and communicated that she had been taken far away from her home and missed her previous owners. She showed me she did not like the new owners as she was left alone a lot, but then she had been moved again.

I asked, "Are you happy where you are now?" and received an enthusiastic response. I felt that she was happy and felt part of the family.

I was really surprised about how much information I had picked up. I had written it all down, ready to discuss it with my friend. He was astonished when I described a dog that he said sounded exactly like Murielle, the poodle. She had been rescued from difficult circumstances and taken to a dog's home, where she proved very wary toward dogs that she did not know and would snap and bare her teeth. He also said that Murielle had very long back legs that were out of proportion to the rest of her body. She would lie down and stretch them right out after a walk, which looked funny. When I told my friend that Murielle wanted to thank him for taking her in, he was clearly moved.

I then told him what I had found out from the other dog, Twinkle. He confirmed that the back door was left open for her, as she loves to go in and out, checking to make sure her owner is still there. Twinkle had been to two or three homes before she was adopted from a local dog rescue. My friend was delighted to hear that Twinkle is happy now and feels part of the family. "We wanted her to feel she belongs with us," I was told, "so we call her by our surname, Twinkle Small."

I was quite taken aback by this and pleased with how well my first attempt at animal communication had gone. I couldn't wait to do it again with another friend's pet.

My response:

Smita's story shows that even if you've never owned an animal, you can still become a pet psychic. The important thing is that you have a genuine love and respect for animals. It takes a bit of courage to discuss the results with the animal owner, but when you do and gain validation, it helps to remove any negative thoughts that can otherwise hold you back.

Trying Different Animals

Asking friends, neighbours or colleagues if you can do a pet reading for them is also important because it opens up the possibility of doing readings for a more diverse range of animals. There are always plenty of cats, dogs and horses to link with, but birds, reptiles, rabbits, hamsters, guinea pigs and even fish will give you a different perspective. Most animals and species tend to be open to the process, although you must never assume that any animal will communicate. That is why we always need to telepathically ask for their permission before commencing.

It is important to take this work at your own pace and only do what feels right for you. We've already seen that many deceased animals want to communicate with their owners in spirit, and if this feels right, you can practise this too, but it is a personal decision so don't rush the process. You are under no obligation to work with anything other than living animals; in fact, many experienced animal communicators or psychics prefer to deal only with the living.

When you offer to do a reading, explain to the owner that you are working to develop your skills and gain valuable experience. Some people are intrigued and curious, some may have already heard about animal communication or even had some previous experience and, happily, you will find most people will give you permission.

Farm Animals

You can also use PACT to practise with animals you come across, whether it's a guinea pig in the pet store, a sheep on a farm or an elephant in a zoo.

Some time ago, I kept some ponies in a field, which they shared with two sheep, Geoff and Mabel. The sheep quickly became familiar with my evening routine of feeding my ponies and would come running over to me when they saw me with a bucket of food. They were always together, so I telepathically asked them how they felt about each other. Mabel sent me a feeling of overwhelming love for Geoff, and Geoff did the same for Mabel. The owner of the field told me that they had been together for 12 years. They had never, ever been apart and hence their close relationship with each other.

Whenever I'm in the countryside and see sheep, cows or even pigs and goats, I like to ask them (telepathically) how they are feeling and if they have anything to tell me. One summer afternoon, my daughter Rachael and I were walking my dogs in the beautiful Malvern Hills in the English countryside. As we got to the top of the hill, there was a herd of cattle separated from the path by an electric fence. I stopped to look over at them, and then in my mind I could hear the words, "Help me, help me." I told Rachael what I could hear in my mind and said I thought that one of the cows must be in trouble.

We rushed over and, as we got closer I could see one of the cows looking very distressed. She was holding her leg up and was unable to put her foot on the ground. This poor cow was obviously in great pain. I telepathically asked her what was wrong, and she told me, "I have an abscess in my foot. Please help me." As we looked around, we saw a notice near the electric fence with a phone number for the local council, so I rang the number, explained I had just seen a cow that was lame and distressed and added that I believed she had an abscess in her foot. The lady I spoke to reassured me that she would contact the owner and call a vet. I then telepathically told the cow that help was on its way. The cow thanked me, and I felt grateful that I had been able to do something to help her.

It can be fascinating to communicate with wild animals as well as domesticated animals. Visit a zoo or wildlife sanctuary, or even go for a walk where there are farm animals on which to practise your skills. Communicate in the same way using the PACT step-by-step technique (see chapter 9).

- Don't forget to introduce yourself at the start and thank the animal at the end.
- What questions can you think of to ask a wild animal or farm animal?
- Does it feel any different from communicating with domestic animals or your own pet?
- How do you feel about not having your findings validated?
- Record your experiences in your journal.

Sceptics

If you tell people you are learning the psychic skills to talk to your own pets, not everyone will be on board, so don't be surprised if you come across disbelievers or sceptics. Try not to take it as a personal attack when someone is not open to your developing skills, is outright rude to you or just thinks the whole idea of talking to animals is a joke. One good way to handle scepticism is to say, "Would you like me to try anyway? I will welcome your honest feedback." I have used this tactic many times and, in almost every case, the sceptical person has agreed.

Many doubters became much more interested when I fed back information they could quickly verify. Of course, you will sometimes encounter someone who is unwilling to participate. In this instance, trust your judgement, accept you will never convince everyone and know when to bow out gracefully.

BETSY, THE MARE

A few years ago, I had a saddlery business providing new and second-hand horse-riding equipment. During this time, I made many business contacts within the saddle-making industry, including a woman called Carol who was a saddler from Walsall, a town in the Midlands in England that was famous for its saddle making. Carol had her own smallholding, kept horses and ponies and worked from home in a workshop in her garden.

One day, I went to Carol's house to collect an order of saddles that she had repaired for me. As we got chatting, Carol told me her mare, Betsy, had started to act strangely and out of character. Carol explained that she'd owned Betsy, who was now ten, since she was a foal and that normally, she was a placid and easy-going horse that was a pleasure to handle and ride.

I decided to tell Carol I was an animal communicator and asked if she'd like me to talk to Betsy to see what was wrong. Carol looked shocked and said, "I'm really surprised that you do this, Beth – you seem such a normal person! I think Betsy is just being naughty and needs discipline."

Carol explained that she'd tried lots of different tactics with Betsy, including using different bits (mouthpieces) on her bridle. She had asked the horse dentist to examine Betsy's teeth and a horse chiropractor to examine her back. A farrier confirmed that her feet were in good condition – so everything checked out physically. Yet she still was behaving oddly, especially after she was tacked up ready for a ride. Carol told me at this point, Betsy would become anxious and make it difficult for Carol to mount her. The horse would move around, paw the ground and sway sideways each time Carol attempted to ride her. It was clear to me that Betsy was trying to show her owner that something was very wrong, but Carol was stumped. So, although still reluctant, she agreed to take me to see Betsy in her paddock.

Betsy was a beautiful bay Welsh Cob pony, measuring 14.2 hands. She came over to the fence to greet us with her ears forward – a sign that she was relaxed. I put my hand out and stroked the side of her face. She stood quietly and began nuzzling my hand. I immediately felt a surge of emotion coming from her as Carol said, "Okay, I think Betsy likes you so I'm willing to give this communication thing a try."

I telepathically introduced myself to Betsy and then started the two-way process of communicating. Betsy gave me mental pictures and words and phrases to describe her life and current situation. I told Carol that Betsy was happy and loved her very much.

Betsy said that Carol would often come and talk to her in her stable and cry into her mane. I shared this information with Carol who looked taken aback but confirmed she'd been really upset lately and had done this. Then Betsy showed me an image of a man and said he had broken Carol's heart. I saw him packing a suitcase and driving off in a sports car, which, again, Carol confirmed.

"But how does Betsy know this?" she asked.

I explained that Betsy was a very sensitive horse with psychic ability and knew a lot about Carol and her life. I could see Carol was no longer a sceptic and was now convinced of the validity of animal communication.

"Please ask her what's wrong and why she doesn't want to be ridden," she said.

Betsy told me her saddle was painful. It leant to the right-hand side when ridden so it felt as though Carol's right leg was longer than her left leg, making her feel unbalanced. Carol, who was a saddler herself remember, felt that couldn't be right, because she would have spotted something like that.

As we chatted over a coffee, Carol said she would check the saddle. The following morning, she rang to say she had asked her daughter to take photos of her sitting in the saddle on Betsy's back and that the photos had shown what the horse had told us: that the fault lay with Carol, who was riding crookedly and leaning to the right.

A couple of weeks later, Carol rang me to say that she had taken a couple of riding lessons with an instructor to correct her posture and riding position, and that Betsy was back to her normal self.

Thanks to that reading, Carol switched from being a sceptic to someone who came to one of my workshops and learned how to communicate telepathically with animals herself. She says, "If you had told me this time last year that I would be able to talk to a cat and know what they are thinking, I wouldn't have believed you! But it's the best thing I've done in a very long time."

JD, THE CAT

Shiva explains:

In 2009, I lost my beautiful cat, JD, to cancer. Naturally I was devastated to have lost him, and getting over his passing wasn't easy, as he had been my loyal companion for over 14 years. He was family. JD was a loving and intelligent soul with beautiful emerald green eyes and a fluffy white coat.

Due to his cancer, JD had developed diabetes, so I had to learn to give him injections daily. He was very understanding and never complained once. On the day of his passing, everything was as usual; he was his happy self, giving me no indication of what was to come.

The hour of his passing came, and he passed peacefully in my arms. I had to tell him it was okay to go. In the midst of sadness and the hole that was forever left in my heart, the dark cloud of guilt was setting in, and I found myself questioning whether I had done everything that I could possibly have done for him

Although a little sceptical, I sent Beth a picture of JD, but that was all. She had no prior knowledge of me or my cat and no way of learning anything about us.

Beth accurately picked up on JD's personality immediately – that he was more like a dog, following me around or sitting by my feet. She described his health issue and his passing and included details that only he could have known.

Then – without any prompting from me, although this was the question I most wanted to ask – Beth said, "JD is saying you did everything that you could for him."

My eyes welled up, and the tears of joy started to roll down my face. He was happy and not alone and all those worries that I had allowed into my mind were baseless. He knew so much about everything that was going on in my heart and life that I knew for sure he was still around me, and that even now, with him in spirit, we really are inseparable.

My response:

Shiva is a scientist by training with an MSc in Organizational Psychology and one in Applied Psychology and so, as she freely admits, she brought a healthy skepticism to our readings.

She had a very strong bond with her cat, JD, and had cared for him during his illness. I could picture how calm he was when she gave him his injections, and when, at the end, she had reassured him that it was okay to go. However, like many owners, the guilt that perhaps she had not done enough for JD had crept up on her. Happily, I was able to reassure her that JD felt and knew she had done all the right things.

Our pets remain spiritually connected to us throughout our lives, and there are no time limits on our ability to communicate with pets that have passed. Shiva still receives messages through readings from JD, 12 years after his death. In one reading he predicted she would offer a loving home to another cat and that prediction gave Shiva the permission she was seeking to allow another cat into her life when the time was right.

What these case studies show is that even when someone says they are sceptical about the validity of animal communication, it does not necessarily mean they are not willing to give it a try. My advice is never to set out to prove anything; just give someone who is sceptical the opportunity to see for themselves.

As the next chapter shows, solving a real-world issue, such as a behavioural problem, can be a sure-fire way to convince a sceptic!

13

How to Solve Pet Problems

Over my years working with animals and people, I have discovered that animal communication can be highly beneficial when there is an unresolved issue with a pet, meaning that an owner is at the end of their tether. Many people have consulted me when they have tried everything else, admitting to me, "You are my last resort." It may be that they have already seen a behaviourist, consulted a vet or other health professional, and yet the problem persists and the cause remains a mystery.

As we have seen from the case studies I am sharing in this book, animals are extremely complex, and so there can be a variety of reasons why they are behaving in a certain way. And it never ceases to amaze me what can be at the root of a problem. It may be that you want to resolve a problem that your own pet is experiencing, or you may want to try to help a friend.

If you are helping a friend, the best starting point with any unresolved behavioural issues is always the owner, who can give you a better understanding of the relationship they have with their pet. Of course, that can call for great tact from you. Owners can be highly sensitive to perceived criticism so you will need to tread lightly when you start to untangle the often complex reasons behind a particular behaviour.

Focus on the Positive

As you might expect, most of the people who contact me to ask me to communicate with their pets usually want me to tell their pet *not* to do something. For example, "Can you tell my dog to stop barking when I leave him at home because my neighbours are complaining about the noise?" or "My horse doesn't like his field mate – can you tell them to make friends with each other?" and I've even had, "My cat likes to stay out all night and I like her to be back at 9pm."

Most animals crave attention but respond better to positive reinforcement techniques rather than negative chastising and unhelpful expressions like "don't do that" or "stop being naughty". The best way to deal with bad behaviour is simply to ignore it and to make sure you praise the behaviour you want instead.

For example, if your cat is peeing on the carpet, verbally telling them off draws attention to this behaviour and therefore encourages the cat to do the same thing over and over again. To praise the cat when it pees in its litter tray or in the garden draws attention to the good behaviour. Most owners will realize that making a fuss of a pet when they behave well is by far the best way to eliminate more problematic behaviour. That said, we can also use our newly developed techniques to support the good behaviour we prefer to see.

Remember, animals are instinctive beings, and there is no guarantee that, just because you can and do communicate telepathically with them, passing on messages and requests from their owners, they will do what the owner wants them to do.

I find it is more helpful to try to get down to the root cause of the problem and then consider small steps that could be taken to initiate positive and lasting changes. Positive change, of course, requires a positive mindset, which makes focusing on negative behaviour counter-intuitive and something that can often make the matter worse. Remember, the animal will be seeing into your mind – in the same way you are seeing into theirs – and translating your thoughts too. So, if you focus solely on "bad behaviour" the animal may misinterpret this focus as a positive and therefore continue to repeat.

Visualize Good Behaviour

If we accept that we create those things we invest our energy in, then by visualizing how we would *like* our pet to behave – rather than how we *don't* want them to behave – we can send them a positive signal that they will respond positively to.

Visualize the behaviour you want, not the behaviour you do not want. Sending images and pictures telepathically to our pets to show them the behaviour we want from them is powerful and enables them to understand our request.

Your dog may be running around excitedly while you are trying to put the lead or harness on before a walk. Mentally send a picture of your dog sitting quietly and calmly allowing you to place their harness and lead on them; this will show them the behaviour you expect from them. It may not work immediately; you will certainly need to practise this technique, but it can really make a difference.

Animals are continually reading our thoughts, so be mindful about the pictures and words that you are focused on when you are in their company. For instance, you may not want your dog to sit on your sofa, so you tell them, verbally, "Don't get on the sofa!" But if, as you are saying this, you have a picture in your mind of them sitting on your sofa, that's what your dog will also see in their mind. And when they see that image, they will think you want them to sit on the sofa and, of course, oblige. Try instead to focus on what you want to happen by seeing a picture in your head of your dog sitting in their own bed, and that's what they will pick up on, understand and do to oblige you.

Until we understand that our pets can read our thoughts, we won't realize that often the real issue is coming not from the pet but from the owner. The poor pet is merely responding to signals from the owner in order to please them and make them happy. It's not their fault they have misinterpreted the image they have picked up on.

Where to Start

You can start a communication that is designed to get to the root cause of behavioural problems in the usual way, using the PACT method (outlined in chapter 9), which will enable you to see if the animal can give a reason or explanation for what is going on. You can think of some relevant questions to put forward or incorporate some of these suggestions.

- Is there something that is making you feel anxious?
- What can tell me about your behaviour?
- Do you feel healthy?
- Can you tell me about what's happening in your life right now?
- Has something changed in your surroundings or home life?
- Do you have a message for me/your owner?

You may have a specific issue you are concerned about and, if so, you can structure your questions accordingly. You may want to send images from your mind to the animal's mind, as well as words and phrases. For example, if your own dog keeps chewing your shoes, picture the shoes in your mind, set the intention the pet will telepathically see the shoes, and then ask a relevant question such as, "Can you tell me about chewing shoes?"

The Root Cause Might be Your Situation

I've also noticed that pets and their owners can be so bonded that animals may demonstrate a certain behaviour when the issue is not theirs at all but one that is facing their owner. I've already said that I believe animals are so psychic that they can see our past, present and even future. So, a behaviour issue may reflect the owner's emotional state of mind, a problem that the owner is dealing with currently or even something that may be a challenge in the future for them.

The root cause of persistent behaviours that an owner may find troublesome is often something they did not expect at all. I recall a reading where a dog started to chew his owner's shoes. The owner thought it was odd behaviour as the dog was six years old by this point and had stopped chewing things several years before. When I asked the dog about this behaviour, I received a surprising answer in the form of words in my mind: "Fear of walking forward." I soon surmised and ascertained that this was more about the owner's life than the dog's.

I asked the owner (tactfully) if he was fearful of progressing in any area of his life, and he revealed he had been made redundant from work. He had just had an interview for a new job, which he had been offered, but he was scared of taking this next step because he had loved his old job and the people that he used to work with and so was sad that he'd had to leave. He told me that he was dreading starting a new job and wondering if he would be any good at it. He then realized it was his old work shoes that his dog had been chewing.

We discussed his fears and worries around work, and I suggested that he contacted a career coach to help with this transition. A month later, he got in touch to tell me his confidence was growing in his new role and that he realized this new challenge was just what he needed.

Oh, and his dog had stopped chewing his shoes!

SIGNPOSTING TO FURTHER HELP

If you manage to pinpoint the root cause of a behaviour problem during a professional reading, you should not only pass this information on to the owner, but also suggest where to go from there if they feel they need further help. This means it is wise to build connections with other reputable professionals in your locale who you would be happy to refer the owner to.

Getting a Message Across

Animals often become very bonded to their owners and even energetically linked, with thoughts from one to the other flowing, mind to mind, even when the owner is not really aware of this. I have learned that one of the most common reasons for an animal to start behaving unusually is when they are trying to get an important message through to their owner. This may be about their health, their wellbeing or simply their likes and dislikes.

As mentioned, I believe animals are psychic and have the ability to see our past, present and future. So a behaviour issue may reflect the owner's emotional state of mind, or a problem that the owner is dealing with.

Another way to look at behaviour issues is to think about what the animal is teaching you. Each animal has a purpose in life, and I believe it's not an accident that you are together.

Recognizing Common Behaviours

Animals can demonstrate similar behaviour when dealing with an issue. As you become more experienced in animal communication, you may want to record the animal behaviours that relate to specific issues. As you become more adept, you can look back and see if you can identify any common patterns. This may be useful when an owner says, "My dog is doing [this]," or "My cat has started doing [that]." You will be able to refer back to previous experiences and consider previous reasons you have identified in relation to this new animal and owner. Have a look at the following case studies to see how animal behaviours might uncover other issues.

The issue surprisingly may not be about themselves; they can be reflecting on what the owner is going through in their lives. Read Benny the Spaniel's story on page 147 to see how this might work in practise.

MURPHY, THE BAY HORSE

Murphy was a large bay horse and a talented showjumper, but his owner, Mary, was frustrated with him, telling me, "Murphy is a brilliant horse and I love him so much, yet when we are showjumping he always refuses at jump number three." This happened at every single show they went to, despite the courses and jumps being different.

I communicated with Murphy and received a message from him that showed me that Mary expected him to refuse

at jump three. He would feel her body tense up as they approached that jump and she would hesitate. Murphy showed me that this was his cue to stop. So, that's what he did because that's what he thought Mary wanted and expected from him.

Mary was fascinated to hear this and admitted it was true. We thought about some strategies to overcome the issue, and I suggested to Mary that she allow someone she trusted to ride Murphy over a course of jumps and to observe what happened.

She contacted me a few days later to say Murphy had been the perfect gentleman and had not refused any jumps when her friend Jack rode him. In fact, he completed a perfect clear round.

I suggested Mary could work with a riding instructor to have some jumping lessons to help her "reset" *her* mind while riding Murphy and to break the pattern of expectation. Mary later confirmed this had worked and Murphy no longer refused any jump.

CASPER, THE HORSE

I once had a phone call from a horse owner called Robert, who couldn't understand why his normally friendly and loving horse, Casper, was agitated all the time and did not want to be ridden. Robert told me, "Casper just keeps staring at me as if he is trying to tell me something.

I know there is something going on, but it's all very puzzling."

As soon as Robert told me this, I heard Casper speaking in my head. He said, "Toothache and jaw pain." I advised Robert to book an equine dentist, not a reading, and he said he would do that and let me know the outcome.

Later that week Robert called again and thanked me. The equine dentist had found an abscess in one of Casper's teeth that was causing pain in his jaw.

Animal Instinct

Animals have strong instincts, and these will take precedence over anything else. We should always keep this fact in mind when we learn to communicate with them, because even though we have domesticated pets over many centuries, these instincts are still a huge part of who they are. It is, of course, perfectly natural and instinctive for a dog to bark when they hear an unusual sound; this acts as a warning to alert us or the pack to a potential threat. But barking can be troublesome, especially if the neighbours complain, so I am often asked to tell a dog to stop barking. My reply is always the same. I tell the owner that I can request that the dog stops barking but that does not mean that they will. I could explain to someone that smoking will damage their health, but that does not necessarily mean they will quit smoking even when they have a good reason. Once again, it's about reinforcing and rewarding the behaviour that we are seeking, rather than focusing on the unwanted behaviour we would like our pet to stop doing.

BENNY, THE SPANIEL

When Jennifer contacted me about her five-year-old spaniel, Benny, she told me they shared a close bond and that he had always been well behaved. Jennifer would walk Benny every morning before leaving for work, check on him at lunchtime and be home by 4pm Monday to Friday. They would then spend the entire weekend together. Jennifer had never had a problem with this routine and neither had Benny. Then, out of the blue, Benny started to show symptoms of extreme separation anxiety.

He started being very destructive during the time he was left alone, and Jennifer started to dread what she would find on her return. Benny chewed through a sofa, ripped up cushions and even knocked over a bookcase. Jennifer had consulted with a dog behaviourist, but the issue remained unresolved and was now so bad she was seriously considering rehoming him.

When I communicated with Benny, he showed me that he enjoyed his life and was very close to Jennifer. I asked him why he was now behaving out of character and so anxious when he was left alone.

Benny put an image of a tall man with dark hair into my mind, and, next to this man, he put an image of Jennifer. I felt overwhelmed with emotion and was nervous and anxious. I knew that the emotional feelings were coming from Benny to alert me to the fear he had of this man. So, I discussed my findings with Jennifer, and I asked her if she knew who the man was.

Jennifer told me that she'd recently been contacted by an ex-boyfriend who wanted them to get back together. He had been physically abusive to her in the past but had told her how sorry he was for that and that he had changed. Jennifer wanted to give him a second chance and had been seeing him again. Things had started well, but recently he'd become controlling again, and Jennifer was scared of him. She felt she was treading on eggshells when he was around, and he had also told her he didn't like Benny. If they were to make a success of their relationship, she would have to get rid of him.

Jennifer was upset and regretted allowing this abusive man back into her life, because she could see he had not changed at all. As we concluded the session, I explained Benny knew what Jennifer was going through and his behaviour was his way of protecting her by showing her that something was wrong in her life. I referred Jennifer to a counselling service and asked her to keep me updated about the situation.

A few weeks later Jennifer called me and said she had told her ex to stay away and never contact her again. As soon as she had done this, Benny stopped his destructive behaviour and went back to being his normal, happy self.

This case study shows how much a pet can know about what is happening in our lives and how strongly connected they are to us emotionally. Your pets can pick up on your feelings and moods and even has the ability to psychically see what is happening in your life.

Ailments in Both Owner and Pet

Animals can also reflect what is going on for us with our health and wellness. Sometimes they even exhibit health symptoms that are similar to their owners. I once did a reading for an owner called Tony, whose springer spaniel, Billy, had developed asthma. Tony explained that he had asthma too. Another time I went to see a woman whose Red Setter, Divo, had slipped a disc in his back. When I arrived, my client's husband was lying on the sofa with … a slipped disc in his back.

From experiences like these, I began to realize the importance of the owner/pet relationship, so that they work through their issues, whether health or behavioural, together.

Obviously, the first port of call for a sick pet is the vet and for the owner, a doctor. But once a diagnosis has been given, you may want to try holistic therapies that both you and your pet can use to support your recovery.

Reiki Healing

Reiki is a Japanese hands-on healing technique which can be used on both people and their animals. The reiki practitioner channels universal healing energy and transfers this through their hands to the owner (or animal) to help rebalance the body and help heal on an energetic level. (See chapter 7 for a more detailed explanation of the importance of our invisible energy bodies.)

Crystal Therapy

Crystals radiate positive energy which can promote relaxation and have a healing effect on the mind and body. So, crystal therapy is another gentle and very natural approach to healing, using different types of crystals that have specific healing properties.

Doga (Dog Yoga)

This is a yoga practice where you invite your dog to share your mat. It is not about getting the dog to copy your yoga postures but more about building trust and sharing a special self-care space. "Doga", as it is sometimes called, can work to increase the loving trust between you.

There are so many different healing systems available to owners – and sometimes to their animals too. If you make sure you are taking care of your own health and wellness, including your chakras, you can investigate more of these options and see which system you feel most drawn to, and which resonates with you most for the benefit of you and your animals.

TOOTS AND KIT LA-KIT

Jayne explains:

I took my first animal communication course with Beth in 2005. After learning about her techniques, we were asked to tune in to some photographs of animals that she had brought with her. I chose a picture of a horse and a picture of a parrot and surprised myself by getting some amazingly accurate results. We were then invited to offer our own animal pictures for a reading.

I gave Beth a photo of my two cats: Toots, who was a small white cat aged three at the time, and Kit la-Kit, who was a black female cat and was four. I had these cats when I was in a relationship with my daughter's father.

Immediately, Beth said there had been a lot of upset in the home and the cats were very emotional about this. I was so shocked, I started to cry and had to leave the room to compose myself. My daughter's dad had been extremely abusive to me — physically, mentally, financially and emotionally. I hadn't ever told anyone and, after we split up, we had nothing more to do with him.

My life changed for the better. I became a police officer and have now worked with victims of domestic abuse for years. What upsets me every time is that the animals in the household are caught in these abusive relationships too. I realize that they feel our pain and are very aware of what is going on in our lives.

My response:

Inevitably, Jayne has brought her own experiences to her role as a police officer supporting victims of domestic violence, and she shows empathy and compassion to both the victims and their pets. This case study highlights that you can never predict what an animal will share with you and shows how helpful it is to have an ethical framework to support your work. It is also essential to remain non-judgemental and to respect confidentiality.

14

Lost and Missing Animals

When your pet is missing, it is really hard not to instantly panic. The first thing to do is to exhaust all practical ways of finding your pet. This may include letting the local vet surgeries and rescue centres know, and posting on social media. There are some great checklists online to ensure you have covered all bases (see Useful Resources).

If a pet remains missing for any period of time, some owners will turn to animal communicators for help and, of course, there have been many success stories where pets have been found and reunited with their distraught owners. If you are asked to undertake this task, be aware it is a very complicated service and one that many animal communicators or pet psychics do not offer, because, while you may be able to help, you can never offer any guarantee of success.

In this chapter we will look at how to help someone locate a missing pet. You can obviously also use these steps if your own pet goes missing.

The first thing owners will usually ask is whether their pet is still alive. In truth, you simply cannot answer that question with any certainty. As you now know, I communicate with animals on both sides of the spiritual plane, but it is not always possible, without validation from an owner, to tell the source of the messages and whether it is coming from this world or the next.

If you do decide to try to help locate a missing animal, it is important you maintain a degree of emotional detachment. When you do reach out telepathically to the pet, do so calmly and gently. You want the animal, who may already be feeling scared, confused and disorientated, to feel calm and reassured when you make contact with them.

Ask the owners for a clear photograph of the missing pet, along with their name and age, as this will assist you in making the telepathic link. Obtain as much information as you can about what happened and the circumstances surrounding the disappearance. You can also ask the owners to describe the pet's personality and, if you can, ascertain whether this is something that has happened before. Get as much information as you can because this not a pet psychic reading – you will be linking to try to track the missing animal in order to reunite them with their owner, so this session is all about exploring where the pet may now be.

Pendulum Dowsing

One of the techniques I favour when searching for a missing animal is the age-old art of pendulum dowsing. It works really well when you want to locate lost objects and get an answer to specific questions.

To use a pendulum to track a missing pet, you will need a map of the area and a dowsing pendulum. You can buy a traditional crystal dowser and use that or, if you prefer, make your own.

MAKE YOUR OWN CRYSTAL PENDULUM

You will need a piece of string about 20cm (8in) long or a necklace chain. Thread or tie a weighted object – such as a wedding ring, a pendant or a house key – through it so that it dangles and swings freely. You could also use a crystal pendulum, in which case always choose one that appeals to you. You may be drawn to a certain colour or shape. Go with your gut intuition to choose the one that feels right.

I have used a crystal dowser made from the crystal carnelian for many years. As soon as I saw it, the deep orange colour attracted me instantly. On one side of the pendulum the carnelian had darker natural markings which resembled an eye. I heard the words in my mind, "the all-seeing eye", as I looked at it, so I knew it was the right one for me, and I have used it ever since. It has been successful on many occasions in helping to locate a missing pet.

Different types of crystals have different qualities. Here are some you can consider for your own dowsing pendulum:

- **Carnelian**: An excellent grounding stone. It is known as a stabilizing stone which will bring calm to any stressful situation. It's a stone of truth and will also bring positivity to you.

- **Turquoise**: This is a beautiful and protective stone which enhances intuition. It has calming properties so can reduce feelings of anxiety.
- **Black tourmaline**: This crystal is known for its protective qualities and its enhancement of emotional wellbeing. It is also known as a very powerful healing stone.
- **Dalmatian jasper**: This crystal enhances telepathic communication so is a popular choice for those working in animal communications.
- **Snowflake obsidian**: This rebalancing crystal helps to reduce fear and enables you to see light in the darkness. It can also help to release feelings of sadness and hurt.
- **Lapis lazuli**: Used to aid communication and increase clairvoyant ability, the beautiful blue lapis is a calming stone which dispels negative thoughts.

How to Dowse

If your pendulum is made from crystal, then it needs to be cleansed before you start using it. To do this, hold the crystal under cold running water for a couple of minutes. Then leave it to dry naturally in either the sunlight or moonlight.

There are now three things that you need to establish when working with your pendulum: you may get a "positive" response, a "negative" response or a "neutral" response. This is normally indicated by how your pendulum swings. For instance, a positive response may be indicated by your pendulum swinging clockwise. A negative response may be indicated by your pendulum swinging anticlockwise. A neutral response may be indicated by your pendulum swinging back and forth. The direction your pendulum swings will be personal to you, which means a clockwise "positive" for one person may be a clockwise "negative" for another. There is no right or wrong; you will get the answers when you hold your pendulum; ask the question and allow it to move naturally.

To get your positive, negative and neutral responses from your pendulum, hold the top of the chain or thread it hangs from with your thumb and forefinger, allowing it to be suspended and still. Now – in your mind, without speaking – ask your pendulum to show you a positive response. The pendulum will start to move. This might be slow at first but trust the process and don't try to move it yourself. Keep your mind calm and focused and observe what the pendulum does. Repeat this process to find out your negative response and your neutral response.

Test out your pendulum's movements by asking a few questions to which you already know the answer. For example, I could ask, "Is my name Mildred?" to get a negative response, then, "Is my name Beth?" to get a positive one. Another alternative is to dowse over a test object such as a key and ask, "Is this a coin?"

You should not even consider dowsing to help find a missing pet until you have become skilled with this technique, and, as ever, practice makes perfect. You can dowse at home by asking someone to hide an object in your home. Once you become proficient with this, you can start to use a map to find objects that have been hidden outside your home. For this, you will need a good and detailed map of your locale.

Focus your mind on the object and look for the positive response to where the object is hidden when the pendulum swings over a particular section of the local map. When you have narrowed down the area, you can take your pendulum with you outside and around your home to help locate the object.

Dowsing over a Map to Find a Missing Pet

Once you have become proficient using these methods, you can dowse over a map in order to try to locate the whereabouts of a missing pet. Find out from the owner the precise area the pet went missing from and start there. You may also want to divide the map into a grid.

- Find a calm and relaxed space. Light a candle and play soothing music in the background, if you like. Use the grounding, protection and opening up methods from chapter 7 before you start.
- Hold the pendulum over different areas, using your dominant hand, and observe what the pendulum does.
- Go over each part of the map slowly. Your pendulum will give a negative or neutral response when you are in the wrong area of the map.
- Keep calm and focused as you do this. Do not try to force the pendulum to move or respond in a certain way. Just keep going over the map and acknowledge any areas that show a positive response.
- Now you can narrow the search area by dowsing in more detail over the part of the map where you had a positive response from the pendulum. This is the information you can then pass on to the owner to help them in their search.

THE MISSING COLLIE

You can, of course, use the map on your smartphone or tablet and then use the zoom function to get even more specific about the location where you are getting a positive response from your pendulum.

I recently helped locate a missing Collie dog doing just that.

First, I got a positive response over a village a few miles from the dog's home and, soon, thanks to being able to zoom in on the map of that village, I was able to narrow the search area down to a local petrol station three miles away from the owner's back garden.

I suggested they move their search to that location, and when they arrived at the petrol station, there was the dog – a little dishevelled but delighted to see them.

The owners were overjoyed to be reunited, and it was a very rewarding moment for me when I learned he was exactly where the pendulum had predicted.

Trust Your Intuition

Your eyes may focus on a certain area while looking at a map, or you may be drawn to a spot on the map. Note this down. This can be your intuition showing you where the pet is.

If the pet has escaped from their garden or home, ask the owner to send you a picture of their home, especially showing the door they use when the pet goes in and out of the home. You can send that image telepathically to the pet (particularly useful when asking cats to return to their home) as it shows them that their owners want them to return.

I also set up an "agreement" with the pet and their owner. I ask the animal what food they would like upon their return, and I ask their owners to honour this and make sure this is what they feed their pet if and when they return home.

Remote Viewing

Cats often have a second home, and some cats will go missing for days at a time. You'll get used to your own cat's wanderings, but if you are worried, here's how to use my PACT technique to locate them.

- Prepare yourself and follow the PACT (chapter 9) to Step 7.
- Ask the lost or missing animal to show you where they are.
- Imagine you are looking through the animal's eyes. Observe the images that come into your mind.
- Notice everything you can about the environment and the surroundings. Is it indoors or outdoors? Are there any people or other animals in that environment? Is there anything specific like a road sign or other landmarks?
- If indoors, can you see any clues to the specific type of property or building? Does it resemble a house? Can you see a garden? Does it look like a veterinary surgery? Or a rescue centre?

Note down everything you are given and report your findings to the owners.

Use the "Golden Cord" Technique

You can send a strong message to a missing animal that their owners are missing them and want them home by using this simply but powerful Golden Cord technique.

Ask the owners of the pet to imagine a golden cord linking directly from their heart to the pet's heart, and then to imagine how strongly that golden cord connects them together.

Now imagine that, as the animal communicator helping to locate a missing pet, you are reeling in that cord and pulling the pet toward their owner.

This sends a strong and clear message to the missing pet that the owner is missing them, loves them and wants them to return.

Ask the Angels

I'm a huge believer in the angelic realm and believe that we all have angels that watch over us and guide us in times of trouble. I believe our pets are supported and watched over by the angels, too. There are 15 different archangels; you can choose your own favourite to work with, but when I'm helping to find a missing pet I mentally ask for Archangel Michael's help as he is known as the angel of protection. I also ask for Archangel Ariel, who is the angel of nature and is associated with locating lost animals and helping them to find their way back home, as well as Archangel Raphael, who is known as the healing angel. The combined energy from these three angels helps to protect, calm and give courage to the missing animal.

Archangel Meditation

- Find a quiet and calm place where you will not be disturbed and set up an altar. This can be a tabletop, a shelf in a cupboard or even (if space is an issue) a small wooden breadboard! You can place a special piece of cloth on the top of the area you have chosen to be the altar.
- Now place a photo of the missing pet on the altar along with a white candle (white represents purity and angelic connections). You may want to use crystals and burn incense too in order to create a sense of ritual and relaxation.
- Light the candle and settle yourself on to a comfortable chair; if your altar is in the bedroom, you can lie on your bed.
- Close your eyes and take several deep breaths. Imagine you are now surrounded by a brilliant ball of white light that covers you from head to toe.
- Now, say in your mind:

Dear Archangel Michael, Archangel Raphael and Archangel Ariel, please connect with me and allow me to receive your love, help and guidance in locating the missing animal [add the animal's name]. Through this invocation, please assist them in finding their way safely home to be reunited with their owners. Allow this to be for the highest will and good of all concerned. Thank you.

- Open your eyes and write down any thoughts that immediately follow, as these can be important messages from the angelic realm.
- Remember angels need your permission to intervene and this method of asking the angels for guidance invites them to step in to assist with the search for a missing pet.

SIDNEY'S STANDOFF

Deb explains:

Beth has saved my sanity numerous times when my cats have either been unwell or have gone off on their extended travels. One time, when my cat Sidney hadn't been seen for ages, I was at my wits' end. After a couple of days, I called Beth and explained this was unusual for him because he would usually come home for dinner or when I called him.

I sent Beth a photo to work with, and she came back quickly to say she had seen Sidney standing on top of a garden table having a standoff with another cat, who was under the table. Beth said, "I'll tell him to be home at 8pm."

I waited anxiously and still there was no sign of Sidney. Then, on the stroke of 8pm, I looked over the fence. There he was, sitting on the neighbours' garden table with their cat underneath. I couldn't believe it! It was exactly how Beth had described it.

Neither cat was willing to move, and Sidney wasn't happy that I went round and fetched him in before he could establish who was boss!

My response:

Sidney had shown me exactly where he was and told me that he didn't feel lost at all. I think he was just giving me a picture of what he was up to. Unlike most lost animals, who often submit messages of disorientation and confusion, Sidney felt quite calm and in control – or at least he was trying to be!

TIA, THE TABBY

Carol explains:

My cat had been missing for six weeks and I was desperate to try to find her, so my friend Deb asked Beth if she could help. "Is it a tabby cat with a white chest?" she asked. I was amazed, as she had just described Tia having never seen even a photo. Beth tuned in to Tia and explained that the reason she'd run away was she'd been scared by something and had bolted. She had ended up a couple of miles away, hungry and disoriented, and couldn't now find her way back home.

"Who has a red front door?" Beth asked, as she could see that Tia would return through a red door. We were both shocked because Deb has a red front door!

Beth sent a message to Tia to help her to calm down and regain her bearings. She also sent a telepathic vision of the red door to Tia as an energy channel for her to find her way home. The following morning, I was sitting in Deb's kitchen when my daughter knocked on the door. Deb ushered her in – with Tia in her arms!

Beth said she would come back through a red door and she did.

We were all flabbergasted. We had almost given up hope of ever seeing her again. Tia was quite thin and a little worse for wear but in fairly good health considering the length of time she had been missing.

She is still happy and at home to this day.

My response:

I could picture Tia as Carol mentioned her. When you open up to the process, this often happens as it gives the animal an opportunity to present themselves. While Deb's cat, Sidney, had felt relaxed, Tia felt nervous, anxious, confused about her whereabouts and very, very hungry. I could feel that within my own body.

It's important to acknowledge how you feel during a reading as this can be a message from the missing pet and will help you to better understand their dilemma. I was able to send messages to Tia as well as receive them, so I sent her a mental image of her family missing her and wanting her to come home, and a picture of the red door to guide her. I was elated to hear from Deb the next day that Tia was back. It is so rewarding when there is a positive outcome.

ANIMAL PROFILE EXERCISE 5

Locating a Missing Animal

Vivienne is a small Chihuahua cross (you met her on page 115). She ran away while in a park after becoming startled by another dog, bolting away from the park onto a busy road. Her owner, Rachael, gave chase but soon lost sight of her. She was lost in one of these cities for two hours, until she was found hiding in a car park.

Below is a dowsing grid showing six cities in the UK, one of which is where Vivienne was lost. Can you discover which city she was lost in by using your pendulum dowser?

Hold your pendulum over each city. You are looking for a positive response over one city.

Dowse over this grid:

Birmingham	**Bath**
London	**Worcester**
Cardiff	**Manchester**

Find out on page 226 whether your dowsing was able to locate the right city.

15

Communicating with Pets in Spirit

Just to recap, a medium is someone who can "receive" information from the world of spirit from those who have passed away. Revisit chapter 5 to remind yourself about how it's possible to communicate through pet mediumship with animals who have died.

This can be a very rewarding process and bring much comfort and validation about life after death to pet owners. It is nothing to be afraid of and, once you have practised a few times, will feel like a very natural process.

What is discussed in this chapter could be applied to yourself, to friends, family and loved ones who you want to help, or to potential clients, if you choose to set up your own business. For more on that, read chapter 16.

COPING WITH THE LOSS OF A PET

We often regard our pets as part of the family, and many people describe their pet as a best friend. Therefore, when a pet passes away, the grief that's experienced can be overwhelming. I have gone through losses with my own animals – including rabbits, guinea pigs, hamsters, dogs, cats, ponies and parrots – so I understand how traumatic and painful it can be. And when we lose a working animal – guide dogs, therapy pets, assistance dogs for the hard of hearing – the loss can be life-changing.

Grief can affect people in many different ways and it can also affect other animals within the household, as animals can also experience feelings of loss and mourning for their friend. We may see behaviour changes: for example, they may go off their food or want to be left alone and in general appear to be sad. Our pets can also mourn the loss of a person. (Part of good pet ownership is to make provision for our pets if anything were to happen to us. This can be discussed with friends and family members. The RSPCA also offers this service.)

When in grief, you may experience difficulty sleeping, brain fog, deep sadness, loneliness or disbelief, anxiety or depression. Some people may even feel guilty that they have grieved more for their pet than for a person that has passed away. Whatever you feel, it is important to acknowledge these feelings.

I recommend Dr Elizabeth Kubler-Ross's 1969 book, *Death and Dying,* to learn more about the stages of grief and how you can support someone through this – if you are offering your services as an animal communicator.

Methods of Connecting with a Deceased Pet

You can conduct a reading with an animal who is now in spirit using a photograph of them or even by using a good description – including their name, breed and colour. Another way to connect is to physically hold an object that belonged to the pet, such as their collar or favourite toy. You may even decide to work using a photograph and an object at the same time.

The technique of making a psychic link with an animal or person who is now in spirit is known as psychometry or object reading. You can try psychometry with one of your own pets that had passed away or ask a friend or family if they would be willing to allow you to practise on one of their pets who has crossed over.

Conducting the Reading

Set up a room or area in which to work. Start by lighting a candle. White candles represent purity and are believed to bring positive energy into the room. You could also burn a sage smudge stick and waft the smoke around the space; this is a Native American tradition known as smudging which cleanses and purifies a space, creating a positive and peaceful environment. It is believed to have healing properties and to enhance intuition.

Think about the lighting in your room before you start the reading. You may find it more conducive to work in a gently lit area with no bright overhead lights, as these can be distracting. You can use pure essential oil in an oil burner or diffuser, which can aid relaxation and further help by setting the right mood for your work. You can also have some relaxation music playing quietly in the background if this helps you get into a calm mindset.

To begin this process, prepare yourself by practising one of the exercises from chapter 7 and allow yourself to reach a calm and relaxed state of meditation. Use the grounding, protection and opening up exercises you have been practising (and remember to close down at the end of the session). Getting into these routines and good habits each time you conduct a reading will start to become more automatic the more you practise.

Use the PACT method (chapter 9), and when you get to Step 7, go within to ask permission from the pet you are attempting to connect with.

You can hold a photograph, look at one on your phone or form a mental picture of the pet in your mind.

If you are using psychometry to help you make the connection, pick up the object and hold it in your hands. You may wish to close your eyes, which will help to block out any distractions and allow you to focus on the thoughts and impressions that will come to you from the object.

Have a pen and a paper ready or even speak your impressions out loud (you could record this on your phone).

Allow the thoughts and words to flow. Don't think about them too much; don't try too hard to understand them, and do not try to force the information, just be open to what information you receive. The following questions can help you to stay open and receptive:

- What is the first thing you feel?
- Do you feel any strong emotions?

- What do you feel about the character and personality of the animal?
- Were they sociable with people or other animals?
- What activities did they enjoy?
- What was their favourite food?
- Did they have any unusual habits?
- Were they anxious or easy-going?
- Did they have another animal as a companion?
- Did they have any health issues or other conditions?

Describe whatever comes into your mind. Do not over-analyse the information you receive; try to keep it pure and unfiltered.

Remember to write things down or make a recording, as it is easy to forget the details of what happened during the reading.

You will, by now, know that self-doubt can creep in when we are communicating with an animal and that some of the messages that come into your mind may feel as though you have imagined them. This is a perfectly normal way to feel afterwards. The imaginative part of the brain is the part that we are using in this process, so trust that this works. Do not expect to see some version of a ghostly animal with your physical eyes; anything you "see" will be in your mind's eye (or what is often called the intuitive third eye).

Symbols and Images

When communicating with animals (or people) who are in spirit, you may also see symbols or images that represent the message the animal wants to share. With time and experience you will come to better understand the meaning of these symbols, so it's important to keep a record of them in your journal.

For example, if I see a white flower, I now know that this means it is someone's anniversary (or this could be a date of a passing). If I see a yellow flower, this means a significant event will happen within the next two weeks, such as a wedding or a holiday. If I see balloons, I know there is a birthday or celebration about to take place. These symbols are individual, so you will soon be interpreting your own set of symbols.

When pets who have passed away connect in this way, they often give details about their passing or messages about events that have taken place since their passing, which also works as validation for you that this connection is real. The thing our pet said would happen did happen! Here is a case study that highlights this aspect of communicating with an animal who is now in spirit.

WINSTON, THE FAMILY DOG

Tina explains:

Our family dog, Winston, had passed a few years previously, and when he made a connection through Beth as she was looking at his photograph, the first thing he mentioned was that we had a new blue porch door, which was correct and great validation for me that the link was real.

Winston passed on a message to say he had seen a mouse in our kitchen in the early hours of the morning. He said the mouse was eating our new dog Lola's food and she was standing watching him. My husband, David, had come down early that morning to get a drink, and he saw exactly that. The mouse had come into our kitchen through the dog flap.

Beth then said that Winston was showing her that my sister from America would come back home to England. This was true, too; she came home because our brother died.

During the reading, Winston predicted that my son would move back home and live with us for two years before moving again, and then he would get married. And, once again, it all came true.

My response:

Animals in the spirit world often share information about what they see going on in their owner's home. Winston was able to pass on accurate details, which not only meant Tina could validate the link and the message, but also showed her that Winston had an afterlife and remained connected to her, which is hugely comforting for all animal lovers to know.

HECTOR, THE ENGLISH POINTER

Rebecca explains:

I first went to get help from Beth for my English Pointer, Hector, who was 13 and suffering from various ailments which limited his mobility. My key objective was to see if

Beth could ask him how he really felt and what, if anything, I could do to help to make the rest of his days as comfortable as possible.

Beth said she was happy to communicate with all my dogs, past and present, so I turned up with three Pointers in tow, plus photos of another Pointer (Hector's sister) and of a Great Dane, both of which had passed away in the previous couple of years.

Beth went into detail about each of their personalities and then, to my astonishment, asked me which of the dogs had suffered ear problems. I could not think of any specific ear-related issue and asked if she could give me any further clue. She focused again, then looked at me quizzically – an expression I'll never forget – and said, "Sewing?" while gesturing the motion of sewing her left ear. She was clearly bemused – I was utterly astounded!

Just after my eighth birthday, my mother had finally conceded and allowed me to have my first dog, an English Bull Terrier called Kes. As an only child, I treated him like my baby brother and adored him. At one point, Kes developed a huge blood blister on his ear and, following the operation to remove it, the vet sewed what looked like large cardigan buttons to either side of his ear to help it heal properly.

Consequently, that one word, "sewing", in the context of an ear complaint, meant so much to me. Beth explained that Kes had never forgotten me and wanted to be part of the session. I had not mentioned him to Beth or taken a photo of him to show her, so my reaction was a mixture of guilt and shocked delight to realize that he was trying to communicate with me after all these years.

After that first reading, Hector soldiered on for another couple of years, but I finally had to make the agonising decision to have him put to sleep in August 2011 after he suffered the canine equivalent of a stroke. For any animal lover, the loss of a pet is deeply distressing, and I can only say that the information that Beth conveyed to me during that difficult time was extremely useful as I could align what she was describing with what I was seeing with Hector's deteriorating condition. The vet came to see him on consecutive days; Hector reacted vehemently when the vet first appeared, but by the time he returned 24 hours later, Hector was ready to go – in line with what Beth had told me just a couple of hours beforehand.

At the time, I was going through a traumatic divorce and so had been even more reliant on Hector as a source of comfort. Given all his ailments, he had lived far longer than I ever expected, but I was still inconsolable at his loss. Following his death, I asked Beth to contact him once again, as I was keen to see if he was all right in the spirit world and still able to communicate with me. It was during this session that he made what became a remarkable prediction.

He told Beth that he had held out for as long as he could for me but that I would be all right from here. He said the divorce would all be sorted by the following May (some nine months in the future) and, while it would be a rollercoaster ride – which it was, it would work out okay for me.

Hector was right, and I have never forgotten the comfort I felt in accepting he could see what lay ahead for me and his reassurance that things would eventually turn out alright.

My response:

Hector was a strong communicator both here on earth as well as in the spirit world. He is an excellent example of how pets and their owners can form a deep bond on a soul level. I believe that Hector used his psychic abilities to help Rebecca through the challenging time of her divorce and he supported her with predictions that came true. He also helped her to follow his advice when he was ready to pass over. I believe that Rebecca dealt with the loss of Hector a little better by having the readings with him before his passing, as it helped her to reach the decision to let him go, which the vet agreed with.

As an animal communicator and pet psychic, I was able to process these messages and pass them on to Rebecca. But, of course, I am only the messenger in circumstances like these; it is always the owner's decision what they do with the information I pass on.

MEG, THE HORSE

Jane explains:

I have had many amazing animal communications through Beth over the years and all have been very emotional. I have lost several dogs and horses.

On one occasion, my sister's beloved horse, Meg (with whom I had such a strong, loving bond), sadly passed away as she was lying on the grass in her paddock. I was with her and, in her last moments, I knelt over her, telling her how much I loved her and always would. As I talked to her and stroked her face, my tears fell and landed just below her eye.

I decided to have a reading with Beth to see if a spirit connection could be made with Meg. I didn't tell Beth any details; I just handed her a photograph.

During the reading, Beth said that Meg was making a link and sending her love to me. Beth then said that Meg was showing her final moments here on earth: I was kneeling over her from above; I was kissing Meg's face and my tears appeared to be running down from Meg's eyes. This was so accurate, and yet no one could have known about it, as it was such a personal moment between me and Meg. Meg also told Beth that we had such a strong love between us that she felt she could pass over now that she had experienced unconditional love. (As she also said, she had worked hard all her life pulling carts before she found solace at my sister's home.)

I'm so happy she got to retire at such a wonderful country home and knew such love in her latter few years. It's good to know that she's happy and at peace where she is now. I felt the reading provided me with closure and helped me to cope with Meg's loss and to remember the happy times we shared.

My response:

When I communicate with animals that have passed away, I often receive information from them about their last memories. By sharing these, they can give their owner validation that they continue to live on in the spirit world. As anyone who has experienced being in the presence of a pet when they cross over will know, we revisit those final moments in our mind time and time again. It can take us a while to start to remember the happy moments we shared.

Connecting to an Animal in the Spirit World Meditation

Have you dreamt about one of your pets that has passed away? This is known as a visitation dream. It feels very real if you have a visitation dream, and you will never forget it; it will remain with you in a comforting way. Unfortunately, we cannot summon these dreams at will, but we can do a lovely healing meditation which will also allow us to connect with a pet that is no longer with us in the physical world but still connected to us from the spirit world.

This meditation can be very emotional, but it can also bring healing and closure, especially if you weren't with your pet at the time of their passing.

- Get comfortable on a chair or bed and settle yourself down, following the procedures you have learnt.

- Close your eyes and take three deep breaths. Give your body permission to relax; allow yourself to sink into the chair or bed. Now imagine a bright, golden, healing light in the shape of an egg that starts at the top of your head and encompasses the whole of your body. You feel safe and protected, with a sense of warmth that radiates from the golden light.
- Now imagine that you are in a woodland area with tall, green trees. The air feels fresh and cool. In the distance you can see a very large tree that has a door in the trunk. Make your way over to the door and open it. As you step inside, you realize that it is an elevator; the door closes and you can feel yourself moving up, getting higher and higher. When you reach the top, the door opens, and you find yourself in a beautiful landscaped garden full of colourful flowers. They smell sweet and fragrant.
- You can see a pond in the middle of the garden with a tall stone fountain. You can hear the trickling sound of the water. You make your way over to the pond and dip your hand into the cool, fresh water. There are several large fish swimming in the pond, and they blow bubbles up to the water's surface as if to greet you.
- As you look around, you see a graceful peacock standing at the side of the fountain. As you gaze at him, he fans his tail feathers and treats you to a magnificent display of his colourful plumage. You are captivated by the colourful feathers of green, gold and blue. You notice that there are several wooden benches situated around the pond. You choose a bench to sit on and, as you approach it, you can see

one of your beloved pets is already there. Your eyes meet and a deep feeling of love and recognition fills your soul.

- You're both delighted to see each other and to reconnect in this special place. Sit with your pet for a while. This is your chance to tell them how much they mean to you and how much you've missed them. Your pet wants to tell you something too; stay open to listening to their loving message and thank them for this opportunity to be together once again.
- Your inner knowing tells you it's time to make your way back. You say goodbye to your pet, and you watch them walk away. You make your way back through the beautiful garden. You can hear the birds singing and feel warm sunlight on your back.
- You open the door to the elevator and step inside. The door closes, and you feel yourself going down. When you reach ground level, the door slides open, and you find yourself back in the woodland. You step back on to the pathway feeling calm and relaxed. Now count down from five to one: five, four, three, two, one. Open your eyes. Allow yourself to adjust to your current surroundings, and have a drink of water.

SIBLINGS SHYLAR AND LUCAS

Allan explains:

In March 2016, we rescued two Dogues de Bordeaux, a brother and sister called Lucas and Shylar. I knew very little

about their past history but, when they came to us, it was clear they needed a lot of care and attention.

When I heard Beth was doing a demonstration locally, we booked tickets and, on our arrival, placed separate photos of Lucas and Shylar in the box from which she would choose photos to read from.

Without looking, Beth pulled out both of our photos separately, then immediately put them together as siblings. The reading that followed was remarkable. Beth described their personalities and their little traits; she even knew that they had no idea how to play with toys.

Beth mentioned that Lucas had a heart issue, something that the vet had confirmed just a few days earlier. She also said that both dogs were very happy that we had adopted them together and that they liked us, which made us smile.

In October 2019 we lost Shylar to a massive heart attack. Lucas was lost for a while, but he still had our Labrador, Bailey, for company. Then, at the end of 2020, we noticed a sudden change in Lucas. He lost a lot of weight to the point where he lost his chain collar on his daily walk. We walked the same route every day and spent weeks looking for it without success.

The vet soon confirmed his heart was failing. Medication helped for a while, but in April 2021 he suffered a heart attack and we had to make the devastating decision to let him go. We were broken.

Had we done the right thing? There were so many questions going on in our heads.

As it happened, I had booked a work-related reading that evening on Beth's radio show. I messaged to say I couldn't face it as we had just lost Lucas, and she messaged back to offer to change it to an animal communication reading instead.

The show began; at one point, Beth started to eat a shortbread biscuit, saying that she wouldn't normally eat them, let alone on air. My wife and I looked at each other with tears in our eyes and both said, "It's Lucas." He would spit other biscuits out until he got his shortbread.

Our reading followed, and Beth described the events of Lucas's passing. It was as if she had been there with us! She also mentioned yellow flowers. I'd had a dream a few days before in which I saw Shylar running around in a field of yellow flowers. Beth also described a man who was looking after the dogs; we both knew she was describing John, my father-in-law.

Beth told us there was no doubt we had absolutely done the right thing to end Lucas's suffering. When the reading ended, we were in floods of tears, but they were tears of relief in learning that we had done the right thing to let him go and that he was being looked after and was reunited with Shylar. I know that Beth had definitely been communicating with Lucas, and the shortbread biscuits were his way of telling us it was him.

The following Saturday, the small replacement chain collar was returned from the vet, along with Lucas's ashes. We were upset that we did not have his original collar with his name tag, as we have always kept these from our lost fur babies, which is a collection of nine now.

I picked his chain up, put it in my pocket and said, "Come on, boy, one last walk," and I took our other two dogs, Bailey and Bonnie, for our daily walk. I walked round in tears and, close to the end of the walk, in the grass right in front of me was Lucas's missing collar. I was speechless. I know Lucas took me to it and very much doubt if it would have happened without Beth contacting Lucas three days earlier. Somehow, dealing with the grief became a little easier.

My response:

I'm often asked to demonstrate animal communication in front of an audience and this allows people to see first-hand how it works and how the animals can connect through a photograph. Lucas and Shylar were able to give excellent evidence that I passed onto Allan and his wife, who quickly verified all the facts.

When Allan had a reading on my radio show, I was looking at a photo of Lucas and jotting down a couple of messages when I had an overwhelming urge to eat a shortbread biscuit! It was so strong that, during an ad break, I found a pack of biscuits and was still eating one when I came back live on air. I apologized to the listeners of the show and explained that I was craving shortbread biscuits; I would not normally eat anything during a broadcast, but it was as though I could not resist. Allan said they knew instantly that it was Lucas and then validated all the messages he sent them.

I believe that Lucas remains connected to his owners and was able to lead Allan to his lost collar. This brought Allan his proof that life continues after death.

Be Mindful of an Owner's Grief

It is very important to understand the feelings of intense grief and loss and to understand the current emotional needs of an owner who asks you to communicate with an animal that has passed, so that you can decide the best and most sensitive way to approach the reading. If, for example, you are asked to do a reading for a pet who has only just died, consider whether it would be helpful to suggest that you wait a few weeks before conducting the reading, which will give the owner time to process their grief.

You may find it useful to chat to the owner about how they are coping and what feelings they are having. Sometimes I have felt that the pet owner would benefit from some emotional support and have suggested that they contact their doctor or an appropriate support group. There are some excellent telephone bereavement services available that many people do not know exist (see Useful Resources). If you live in another part of the world, you can ask your vet or doctor to recommend similar reputable support groups in your area so that you can then recommend these to grieving owners.

When you agree to communicate with a pet that is now in spirit, it is important that you think carefully about the words and statements you use. Avoid using common expressions such as, "They are in a better place now," or "At least they are out of pain," or "They are no longer suffering." Acknowledge the person's grief, and do not tell them what they should or shouldn't do or feel. Each person will react in their own way. Remain non-judgemental and reassure them that anything that they tell you will be held in confidence. (The exception to this is if you believe that a bereaved owner is feeling suicidal or will harm themselves or someone else, in which case you have a duty to report your concern to the relevant authorities.)

As you begin, it's important that you first find evidence that establishes that you have made a connection to the specific animal. You will need to provide information that the owner understands and can validate, so, as with all the information you may get in this reading, take care to handle this information sensitively.

Most people who ask for this type of reading will see it as an opportunity to tell the animal how much they are loved and how much they are missed, so make sure you send this information to the animal you are linking with.

If you struggle to understand the meaning of the symbols which may arise (pages 173–174), then simply ask the owner what the symbol means to them. You need to practise this first with a friend's pet so you can get used to this dialogue and become comfortable presenting such symbolic messages and asking what information they recognize from your findings.

ANIMAL PROFILE EXERCISE 6

Cindy

This is a picture of Cindy, who passed away when she was 14 years old. See what information Cindy is able to pass on to you. (Remember to ask for her permission before you start.) Check your answers against those on page 226.

Here are some questions you can ask her, or think of your own:

- Can you tell me about yourself and your personality?
- Can you tell me about your background?

- Did you have any animal friends?
- What were your favourite things to do?
- What did you enjoy eating?
- What happened at the end of your life?
- Do you have any advice for me?

Remember to thank her for communicating with you and close down.

A Note on Spirit Guides

I want to touch on the notion of spirit guides, as you may become aware of them as your psychic skills develop.

When we practise this important work of communicating with animals and working psychically to ask what they want and need from those charged with their care, we may find we are not working alone. There is no need to feel any alarm about the idea of a spirit guide who may show up to help you in this work – this will always be a benevolent presence who only has your best interests and that of the animals you are communicating with in mind. And, just as importantly, these guides know not to show up until you are ready and have invited them to help you. Plus, communication with your spirit guide will help you hone your non-verbal communication yet further.

You can think of a spirit guide as being an "entity" that lives on the other side of life – not unlike a guardian angel. Their sole purpose is a loving one; they will guide and support you and share enlightening information to assist you and others you might work with. But, as I've said, they will generally wait for an invitation from you to step into that invisible space where you will be doing this important work. Often, they make themselves known when you take part in a guided meditation that has been designed to help you meet them. They understand this as an invitation from you.

These beings, who will all have once lived an earthly life themselves, are assigned to you at birth. They can be male or female; they can come from any walk of life and from any era. The important thing is that they have agreed to support you throughout your life. Once you have welcomed them and thanked them for making themselves known to you and for helping you with your psychic work, you can ask them their name, which you will hear clairaudiently in your mind. You may have one or more guides who will connect to you at different points in your life, during those times and situations when you most need them. You may have one who stays for a while and then leaves to make way for a new guide. All that really matters is that you stay open to their presence, their guidance, their teachings and their help in your own life and in the psychic work you are choosing to do with animals.

Animal Spirit Guides

While some of your spirit guides will present themselves on two legs and in human form, you will, sooner or later, likely also meet your wonderful animal spirit guides. These are known as totem animals or power animals, and you can learn much wisdom from understanding what a spirit animal means and why they have shown up in your life.

The history of power animals (or animal spirit guides) has its origins in the tradition of Shamanism, which is an ancient healing tradition. Shamans participate in deeply meaningful spiritual practices which are connected to nature. A shaman learns to access an altered state of awareness in order to receive healing, teaching and guidance from their guides. Their dedicated power animal travels alongside them when they go on a Shamanic journey.

It is said that we all have nine animal totems or animal guides through our lives, but you do not need to be a Shaman in order to meet them. Again, upon an invitation from you, they will appear during meditation and other spiritual work. If you are ready now to meet your animal guide, then you can try this wonderful meditation. If you want to wait, you can always come back to this at a later stage when you are further and deeper into your animal communication practice.

Animal Spirit Guide Meditation

Here is a meditation exercise to help you meet your animal spirit guide. Once you connect with them, you may find them to be a helping force as you move forward, as they can act in ways beyond our own abilities.

- Start in a safe and comfortable space, as usual.
- Close your eyes and take in a deep breath to the count of five. Hold the breath to the count of five, then exhale to

the count of five. Do this three more times and allow your body to sink into the chair or bed.

- Now imagine that you are breathing in beautiful white light from the universe. Sense and feel this white light descending down over your head and neck and completely surrounding your body. Know that this is a protective light. Imagine all the stress, worries and concerns that you have are now leaving your body. Imagine, when you breathe in, you are breathing in positive energy and, when you breathe out, you are breathing out negativity.
- Allow the feelings of deep relaxation to flow through your body. Allow any tension to fade away; feel it leave your body all the way from the top of your head to the tip of all your toes.
- Now imagine that you are standing at the top of a grassy hill. When you are ready, begin to walk down this hill. You are walking barefoot, and you can feel the cold grass beneath your feet. As you make your way down the hill, you can see a wooded area at the bottom.
- You find yourself walking through the wood, gazing up at some of the tallest trees you have ever seen. You decide to follow a pathway ahead and, as you make your way along that path, you can see a tree stump in the distance. You walk to the tree stump and sit down to rest.
- You are feeling calm, relaxed and safe among the surrounding protective trees. Then, you hear a gentle rustling sound in the trees and, before you know it, your animal spirit guide is standing in front of you.

- This may be a wild animal or even one of your own pets that has crossed over into the spirit world.
- Greet your guide and ask them if they have any advice for you. Acknowledge the response that comes into your mind. You may also ask if they have any messages for you. When you feel this first visit is over, thank them for joining you.
- Visualize yourself now getting up from the tree stump and walking back through the woods and back up the grassy hill. When you reach the top, it is time to come home.
- Count down from five to one and, when you are ready, open your eyes.
- You may wish to write down any messages that you received during this meditation. Allow yourself to readjust to your waking world, and have a drink of water before you continue with the rest of your day.

PART 3

Using and Furthering Your Skills

As you become established as an animal communicator, opportunities will open up for you on all sides, and you may need to start to make some choices about where you go from here.

For some people, being able to connect with their own pets in an intuitive way is rewarding and life-changing in itself. Those people may be satisfied with their progress and not feel the need to investigate further. Other people will find that this has only whetted their appetite for more knowledge and understanding. This may take one or more of many different routes:

- Offering animal communication services to others.
- Delving further into psychic matters.
- Investing time and energy into counselling courses and training.
- Researching and training in holistic therapies.

These are just a few of your choices – investigate and go with what sparks your interest.

16

Becoming a Professional

It may be that after lots of practice, you decide you'd like to commit to doing readings for members of the public. If so, it is important to work ethically, legally and within current legislation.

Currently, worldwide, there are no specific governing bodies or associations and no formal qualifications that you are required to take, which means anyone can call themselves a pet psychic, an animal communicator or a medium. I believe, because of this, it is of even greater importance that you set and maintain your own high standards and that you always respect the fact that this work comes with considerable responsibility for yourself, your clients and their pets.

Code of Ethics for Animal Communication and Pet Psychic Work

Here is my own code of ethics that I strive to meet and maintain. It provides a framework of good practice standards that you can adapt and personalize to meet your particular requirements. I encourage you to follow these guidelines and always work in a fair and ethical manner to maintain the highest of professional standards.

- **Confidentiality**: Respect the privacy of your clients by keeping all their information confidential. If any records or notes are kept, make sure they are safely stored in a locked cupboard or protected on your computer. You could use encrypted files or a coded system or only use your clients' first names to protect their identity.
- **Data protection**: Investigate the current regulations in your country of residence regarding the storing of data about your clients and its use for marketing purposes.
- **Exceptional circumstances**: In exceptional circumstances, for example if you feel the client is in danger of harming themselves, another person or an animal, then you may override client confidentiality in order to report the case to the police or to a relevant organization.
- **Be non-judgemental**: Do not impose your opinions, values or morals onto another person.
- **Health**: Do not make a diagnosis or prognosis about the state of an animal's health. Refer your client to the vet if you have any concerns. Never promise a cure for any health or behavioural issue.
- **Empathy**: Always show empathy, respect and compassion to your clients and their animals.
- **Limitations**: Work within your limits, honestly and to the best of your ability. If you feel out of your depth, then refer your client to another relevant professional.

- **Legal boundaries**: Look up the current legislation and trade descriptions rules in your country of residence, and work within these boundaries, making sure to keep your knowledge up to date.
- **Costs**: Set reasonable fees; make them clear before you start, and avoid any hidden costs. Offer a refund if someone is dissatisfied, or if you are unable to provide the service they booked. Have a cancellation policy that offers reasonable flexibility to the client while protecting you from clients changing their minds on a whim.
- **Preparation**: Explain what you will do, how long it will take, the cost and the procedure before you take and confirm a booking. You should specify that your readings are "for entertainment purposes only".[1]
- **Conduct**: Always behave in an honest and trustworthy manner and remain fair and impartial.
- **Personal development**: Keep your skills and knowledge up to date by keeping abreast of relevant research, reading around the topic and undertaking further training courses.
- **Responsibility**: Deliver your messages and findings in a thoughtful and responsible manner, taking account of the impact they could have. Explain to your client that they retain personal responsibility for any action taken as a result of the reading.
- **Insurance**: Have appropriate insurance for your work. Consider third party liability if you have people visiting

1 It is the intention to bring spiritual services under the umbrella of consumer legislation in the UK. Before any spiritual service is provided, it must be made clear to the client that it is for "entertainment purposes only".

your home and appropriate cover if you are visiting animals in their environment.

- **Fairness**: Treat everyone in a fair and respectful manner, regardless of age, race, sexuality, disability or religion.
- **Age**: Do not offer readings to clients under the age of 18.
- **Outcome**: Do not promise success or any particular outcome.
- **Other professionals**: Create good working practices alongside other professionals with comparable ethical standards.
- **Veterinary Surgeons Act**: If you are practising in the UK, then you must work within the Veterinary Surgeons Act at all times. Check the rules and regulations for animal welfare if you are living in and/or working in another country.[2]
- **Appropriate local restrictions**: Make sure the regulations you follow are appropriate for your location, as they will vary in different countries and regions.

I have included some useful organizations in Useful Resources, where you can further research these guidelines.

Preparing for a Professional Reading

You should only embark on a professional career as an animal communicator once you have had a lot of experience of validated readings. By that time, you will have developed a preparation routine, and the PACT steps will be second nature.

---

2 Under the Veterinary Surgeons Act 1966, you are not allowed to make a diagnosis or prognosis about an animal's health in the UK.
Read the full legislation at www.rcvs.org.uk

This is a checklist of the procedures you should have in place before confirming a booking.

- **Appointment**: Fix the date, time and location of your appointment. The duration of the reading should be 30 minutes to one hour. I would advise not to go on any longer than one hour as you may find it tiring. Make sure the client knows the timings.
- **Expectation**: Make sure you have fulfilled all the legal requirements in terms of the information to supply to your client, including what to expect, restrictions and legalities. Explain the procedure and that they will have a chance to ask questions after the reading.
- **In person or photographic**: Agree whether this will be an in-person or photographic reading and make clear the requirements of images to be supplied.
- **Safety issues**: If you are doing a reading in person, discuss care and common sense precautions with the owner, and always protect your own safety at all times. Always let someone know where you are going; take a cellphone, and, if you have any concerns at all, consider taking a friend along with you. Remember, animals can be unpredictable at times. For instance, if you are unused to handling horses, then communicate with them safely over a stable door or fence.
- **Information**: It can be helpful to know the animal's name and, possibly, their age beforehand, so you can refer to them easily. This can help you to establish a connection with them. Do not ask for any other information, as it may cloud your judgement.

Don't Complicate the Message

It is really important to keep the message pure, to relay it to an owner just as you heard or were given it, and allow them to validate your information. That way, you allow the client to interpret the message rather than overlaying it with your own interpretation, which may be wrong. If, for instance, you see an image of an oven, just tell the owner what you saw. If you suggest that their pet must have found a lovely warm place by the oven, you will be way off track, if what has actually happened is the recent delivery of a new oven to the family kitchen. Once you begin to get validations of what you have experienced, you will lose the self-doubt that is inevitably part of the initial stages of the learning process.

Pros and Cons of Working in Animal Communication

If you do decide to pursue a career in animal communication, do take the time to think carefully about all aspects of the work, how it will fit in with your lifestyle, how it will impact on your partner or your family. Don't forget that when you are dealing with intuition and emotion, the moments that are joyous and satisfying will be counterbalanced by times that are tiring and upsetting. You will need to be able to show empathy toward your clients but, at the same time, keep a slight distance from their problems. You will not be able to help anyone if you take on the negative emotions of everyone who comes your way – and their pets!

Take a look at some of the ups and downs you might expect, and think carefully about how they might impact on you and how you would deal with them. In each case, I have suggested one way these advantages might be of practical benefit in your life; you may think of others. Write down your thoughts in your journal.

Advantages of Working In Animal Communication	Primary Benefits
You discover your life's purpose.	You may feel you have been marking time until you made this discovery.
It brings you a sense of knowing and belonging.	Relish being part of a community.
You feel connected to your real, authentic self.	We all need to be true to ourselves.
Your empathy with others is heightened.	You will really understand what makes other people tick.
Your work strengthens your belief in an afterlife.	Spiritual strength is a great comfort to many people.
You see situations with more clarity.	This will aid problem-solving and make your life run more smoothly.
You are open to new possibilities.	Expanding knowledge is always rewarding.
New opportunities arise for you.	If you are open to new things, they are more likely to come your way.

Continued overleaf

Advantages of Working in Animal Communication	Primary Benefits
New people and new friends with similar interests come into your life.	Everyone needs good friends.
A positive media interest surrounds you.	This could help you to expand your business.
Social media postings are complimentary.	Enjoy them.
You learn to be non-judgemental about other people.	It does not help to judge other people.
You can work from home.	Benefit from a flexible working life.
Helping others gives you a sense of achievement.	How rewarding is that?!

On the other hand, there are downsides, which you should also consider. Here are a few common problems experienced by people working in animal communication. Again, I have suggested one way of dealing with each issue, but they may not be the best ones for you. Think about the pros and cons carefully and write yourself some notes and suggestions in your journal. Your solutions will be unique to you.

Disadvantages of Working in Animal Communication	One Way of Dealing with the Issue
Family, friends or colleagues may not understand the subject.	Be willing to explain what you do and discuss their scepticism amicably. You may have to agree to disagree.
People close to you – or even people you don't know – might suggest you have "lost the plot".	You know they are wrong. Trust in yourself.

Disadvantages of Working in Animal Communication	One Way of Dealing with the Issue
You might get unwanted attention from the media.	Try to turn it to your advantage by offering to demonstrate your skills. Alternatively, ignore them; they will soon move on to the next story if you remain impassive.
Social media postings could be negative.	Don't read them and don't respond to them. Block the senders and, in extreme cases, report them to the relevant media platform.
Other people might assume you can take on and solve all their problems for them.	Take a professional approach to the services you offer so that the client understands the potential and the limits.
You may be expected to be on call 24/7.	Make your hours of business quite clear. Have a designated "work" phone and switch it off out of hours so it goes to a firm but friendly voicemail message.
People may make unreasonable requests of you, such as telephoning in the middle of the night.	As above!
Some people may expect you to carry out your work free of charge.	Explain your charges up front and make clear any free services you may offer, such as help with locating missing animals. Be professional. This is your job, the way you earn your living, not a hobby.
You may receive invitations to events where the host only wants to show you off to their friends and provide the entertainment.	Have a standing charge for a professional demonstration which you can offer at the same time as you politely decline the invitation.

Continued overleaf

Disadvantages of Working in Animal Communication	One Way of Dealing with the Issue
Ignorant people who see you as different could resort to insults or bullying, either in person or online.	By definition, bullies are weak and ignorant. They pick on you because they don't understand what you do. Report any abusive comments to the appropriate authority and don't let them upset you.
You could be held responsible if you are unable to solve a problem.	Make it quite clear what you can and cannot do and do not foster unrealistic expectations. You might investigate professional insurance; take expert advice.
You might try to empathize too strongly and negatively impact your own wellbeing.	You need to exercise a professional distance. Watch out for times when you feel you are taking other people's problems on as your own and teach yourself to back off. Enlist help if you need it.

Build Your Network

When working as an animal communicator or pet psychic, it can feel a little isolating at times, especially if you are doing readings from home. So, if you are looking for a career change and you are contemplating working for yourself, it's important to consider getting into a good routine and making links with people working in a similar industry.

It can be beneficial to look at what is going on in your area. There are many mind, body and spirit fairs that are advertised locally and over social media. By attending these, you will meet new people who are also interested in these subjects. You may also discover more training opportunities and other therapies that you were previously unaware of.

People who work in a spiritual way tend to be friendly and helpful and keen to share with you what they have to offer. Collect business cards when you are networking so you build up a collection of contact details and social media accounts that you can follow. You can follow these up after the event and make new connections.

Another way to expand your knowledge is to attend a demonstration of psychic skills or mediumship. Many clairvoyants and mediums offer this. You can then witness how someone demonstrates their abilities and how they connect to their audience. A lot can be learned about confidence, style and presentation, and you may even be picked out for a reading!

Referring Clients to Other Services

If you are thinking of practising as a professional pet psychic, it is worth your while doing a little research into local practitioners so that you can make referrals to your clients when the issues that come up during a session go beyond your own expertise as an animal communicator.

This was the case with Jennifer, whose story I shared earlier, who needed to escape an abusive relationship and whose dog, Benny, had worked so hard to protect her and to signal his concerns to her. I did not try to counsel her myself but referred Jennifer to a qualified counsellor who could support her through that transition.

Maintain Your Principles

Whichever direction you decide to pursue, remember to stay grounded, real and authentic while continuing your psychic development. Here are some important factors to remember:

- Developing your gifts does not make you superior to anyone else.
- Do not allow your abilities to go to your head and swell your ego.
- Your skills are a gift which can benefit both yourself and others – use them wisely.
- You should always act with the very best of intentions to all concerned.
- Respect other people's opinions, just as you expect them to respect yours. Do not attempt to force your views on anyone else.
- Always respect the confidentiality of anyone you deal with. Clients may confide personal details to you, or you may discover them during readings.
- Never discuss one client with another.
- Always follow the procedures you have learnt in this book of grounding, protection, opening up and closing down when you undertake psychic exercises or readings.
- Never stop expanding your knowledge; there is always more to learn.
- Show gratitude for your abilities.
- Meditate regularly.

- Be honest. No one knows everything; if you don't know something, admit it rather than guessing.
- Keep yourself up to date with news, laws and the regulations in force in your country of residence surrounding psychic work.
- Learn how to say "no" if people become unreasonably demanding of your time and attention.
- Work within your limits and do not overstretch yourself.
- Set yourself some boundaries to work within, including your availability and the length of your readings.

Working as a professional pet communicator can be hugely rewarding, both for you and those you help. But it does come with a significant moral duty, so make sure you reflect fully on everything in this chapter before making any big decisions. With great power comes great responsibility!

Always remember to work to the best of your ability. If you wish to pursue this work in a professional capacity, you will need to work within current legislation, which will differ depending on where you live. Make it a habit to regularly check legal requirements and keep insurances up to date.

Look After Your Mental Health

To offer animal communication as a service, it's crucial to look after your own health and mental wellbeing. During a reading, you will be getting to know the owner – whether they are worried about their pet's behaviour or grieving a pet that has passed or fearing the worst if a pet is missing. It can be extremely emotionally draining to deliver often important, life-changing messages to a client. Therefore, you need to maintain good mental health – here are some of the things I focus on:

- **Manage your stress levels**: Consider counselling or practise relaxation and mindfulness. Talk to your doctor if you feel stress is affecting your life.
- **Practise gratitude**: Being grateful and appreciating what you have will not only raise your energy vibration but also allow more of it to flow effortlessly into your life.
- **Practise kindness**: Acts of kindness have a ripple effect: the more you act kindly, the more people you reach with your kindness, and the more people who will pass it on.
- **Practise forgiveness**: Forgiveness is not about forgetting what has taken place. It's about releasing yourself from the negativity it causes, such as anger, vengeance and resentment.
- **Get outdoors and move your body**: Breathe in fresh air, ground yourself by connecting with nature and do some physical activity.
- **Watch your language**: Speak kindly to yourself. Don't put yourself down with negative comments. Be grateful for the person you have become and appreciate your unique qualities.

It's also important to note that animals can instinctively pick up on our moods and health issues, both physically and mentally, and being in a good space means you can be the most help to the owners – you will not be clouding the communication with any issues you are working through.

17

Further Training

There are lots of opportunities for you to explore your capabilities and potential through workshops and training courses. These can expand your knowledge, improve self-esteem and increase confidence. It's good practice to set aside some time for self-improvement and awareness, even if it's as simple as reading a book or regular meditation. Look at the following forms of training and therapy, and see if any appeal to you as potential future avenues.

Training as an Animal Grief Counsellor

Assisting someone through the grieving process can bring much comfort and help to those suffering from the loss of their pet, which can feel just as devastating as a human loss. Pet bereavement counsellors are often employed by animal charities and veterinary surgeries, or this may be something that you might want to do on a self-employed basis. It can help you with animal communication readings, too, as it will teach you how to react to those experiencing grief and how best to offer support.

Tellington TTouch Training

The Tellington TTouch was developed by Linda Tellington Jones over 40 years ago. It is suitable for use on horses, dogs and other animals, as well as people. It is a gentle training method that develops trust and honours the mind, body and spirit of animals and their owners. It includes a circular touching technique, the benefits of which include lowering stress levels and aiding relaxation. It is based on a mindful approach, when working with animals, and provides a gentle and effective way to increase your self-confidence to help solve behavioural issues. There are more than 1,600 certified practitioners in 41 countries around the world. Tellington TTouch has its own YouTube channel, which provides demonstrations, further information and instructional content.

Canine Massage Therapy

This hands-on therapy assists the overall wellbeing of dogs. It is a non-invasive therapy and can help induce relaxation, relax muscle spasms and tension, accelerate recovery from injuries, help maintain flexibility and support the immune system. This treatment can give relief from aches and pains, improve skin and coat condition, reduce stiffness and increase range of movement in joints, so it is much appreciated by more senior dogs.

Equine-Assisted Therapy

Horses are sensitive animals and are highly perceptive; they respond to body language and have a highly developed sense of awareness. This therapy, which has its roots in combined psychotherapy, can be used to help people with addictions, mental health issues, behavioural issues and emotional issues. It can also help improve self-esteem. Participants engage in activities with horses and are required to use their own initiative to problem-solve, therefore making them accountable for the results. There is no horse riding involved. Sessions are structured to address the clients' needs. Training courses are available around the world.

Counselling Training

In this field, you can focus on both people and animals. I discovered that many people will open up to you about their own personal issues while doing a reading focused around their pet. The client may start to "offload" and talk about their fears and concerns for the future. I have encountered this on numerous occasions and felt that, with more training, I could do more to help, so I decided to attend counselling courses, as I wanted to give the very best service to my clients in a professional way.

Counselling training enables you to understand how and why to approach other people's difficulties so that you can open up their field of opportunity to take action to solve the problem. Counselling looks at self-development as well as how you can assist others. You can see if there are any counselling courses at your local college. You can also search the web for online counselling courses.

Final Thoughts

I hope this book has given you plenty of inspiration and encouraged you to explore all aspects of being an animal communicator and pet psychic. The key message is to trust in your own capabilities and to trust the process.

PACT is my tried-and-tested method of accessing true spiritual connections to animals. Learn this, and you will come to understand that the animals will guide you and will not let you down.

There are plenty of exercises for you to revisit, giving you the tools to practise everything you have learned so far, and you can also review the case studies to confirm how they authenticate this process. Use them to motivate you during your development.

Being an animal communicator and pet psychic can open many new doors for you. We have looked at reuniting lost pets with their owners, and I have shared my knowledge of psychic practices that can enhance your intuition and broaden your horizons. Revisit the tips and advice to help you to develop a healthy mindset and continue to explore the many techniques shared with you to assist you on your communication journey.

Every animal you encounter will have something new to share and a special lesson to teach you. There will be highs and lows on your journey. I believe in the power of synchronicity, and you may often find yourself in situations that seem predestined. Don't be surprised if people start chatting to you about their pets – from strangers you meet at the supermarket to people you encounter in day-to-day situations. After you have been learning about animal communication, these moments and conversations seem to present themselves to you, so stay open to hearing them; it's as though people subconsciously know that you will understand. Offer your support, show empathy and practise kindness by actively listening to those who feel they need to share their current situation about their pet with someone who is compassionate. Do remember, though, there is a time and a place when it is appropriate to use animal communication skills.

By now, you may be keen to explore the subject further; plenty of experience can be gained by connecting with like-minded people and doing your own research. A lot can be learned by observing other animal communicators and pet psychics; noticing their unique ways of working will help you to establish your own style. I would suggest you continue a regular meditation practice and make sure you keep using your journal to note down how you feel and what new experiences you encounter.

I have learnt how to attract some wonderful people and manifest great opportunities into my life as I follow animals' guidance and wisdom. I have become more "dog": sniffing out more information and being enthusiastic about meeting new people. I have become more "cat": retaining my independence and no longer worrying about what others think. I have become more "horse": embracing a sense of freedom and jumping over obstacles when they have presented themselves. I have become more "bird": enabling me to look at life from a new perspective and spreading my wings as far as possible. I have become more "fish": going with the flow. Embrace the teachings each animal can bring to you.

Throughout this journey, I have been lucky to have been supported by my loyal family and friends, who have never judged me or tried to stop what I do. I have been offered many wonderful opportunities to be featured in the media, which I am truly grateful for, and I have made some true friends along the way. With this, I have made lasting connections to some very special pet parents and, of course, their pets.

You never know where this journey will take you, especially when you are passionate enough to want to enlighten others about the secrets of pet psychic communication. I hope you will continue to communicate with many more animals that come into your life.

If you embrace this way of life, you will never stop learning and you will never be bored. You may delve into subjects that you never knew existed. Have the courage to share this knowledge with others in order to help as many pets and animals as you can. You never know where this path will lead you, but I can honestly say your life will never be the same again.

Animal Profile Exercise Results

Here are the results of the questions I asked in the animal profile exercises. You can use these answers to check how successful you were in making a telepathic link with the animals.

Exercise 1 – Monty

Did you make a strong connection with Monty (page 112)? How much of your information can you now validate?

- Monty was rescued when he was two days old, along with his sister Minnie.
- Monty and Minnie were adopted by a family with two teenage children, Hannah and Sophie. Monty is a confident cat who loves to be outside. He often will stay away from home overnight or for two or three days. Monty is a hunter; he often catches birds and mice.
- Monty is described by his owners as playful, moody and cheeky. He enjoys a fuss and the occasional cuddle.
- Monty loves to go to the cattery while his owners go on holiday. He seems to act differently there, becoming very affectionate with the lady who runs it.

- In 2018 Monty was attacked by a fox and was treated at the vets for two puncture wounds on his back leg. They required stitches.
- Sadly, Monty's sister, Minnie, passed away in 2018 while at the vets being treated for an abscess under her chin.
- Monty's favourite foods are fish and yoghurt.

Exercise 2 – Claude

Did you manage to make a connection with Claude (page 114)? How do your answers compare with his history?

- Claude lives with Rachel and Jonny in London, England. He is a rescue cat who was found as a stray, and they adopted him from Cats Protection. Claude is affectionate and likes to be physically close to his owners.
- He is very vocal and makes lots of noise, especially at mealtimes.
- Claude is very food-orientated and always finishes his meals. He can scavenge for food and visits another house in the road to steal their cat's food! One of his favourite foods is yoghurt.
- Claude has been diagnosed with stress and anxiety by the vet. He gets distressed in a cat carrier and dislikes car journeys. His owners provide a Feliway cat plug to alleviate his stress.

- Claude loves toys and his favourites include cat springs and stuffed fish.
- He enjoys sitting on his owner's laptop and likes being outside in the garden climbing trees.
- He stays within the local vicinity and comes home when called. He regularly loses his collar.

Exercise 3 – The Three Dogs

How much did you pick up about each dog (page 115)?

Misty

- Misty is a rescue dog from Poland, and she has had her name changed.
- At around ten years old, Misty is the oldest of the three dogs and was used as a breeding bitch before she was brought over to the UK.
- Misty loves food and is very greedy, but she refuses to eat rice.
- Misty has had several bouts of gastroenteritis.
- She wears a red coat in cold weather and is a loving and kind dog who loves her comforts, visibly displaying excitement when she sees a blanket.
- Her owners joke about how she stretches out her long legs when resting, and she is known to flop her whole body down onto comfortable textiles, much to her family's amusement.

Vivienne

- Vivienne is a rescue dog and is the most dominant and bossy of the three in the photograph.
- Her name has been changed from her previous name, Princess. Vivienne is the youngest of the three dogs at three years of age.
- Vivienne is a very energetic and lively dog who lives in London.
- She has a tendency to bark and bite the vacuum cleaner when she is not otherwise playing tug of war or chewing her soft toys, her favourites being cuddly grey sloths.
- Vivienne enjoys participating in dog yoga, also known as Doga, and travels regularly, often going on the London Underground or across the UK by train. Tube/train travel does not affect her, although she is known to experience car sickness.

Tilly

- Tilly is a quiet and friendly girl who has had her front teeth removed.
- Tilly suffers from an ingrown claw, so her claws are trimmed regularly.
- Tilly bonds well with other dogs, although she can be nervous and is frightened of newspapers.
- Tilly often likes to hide in small spaces and loves to play with Vivienne; their favourite game is often referred to as "crocodiles".

Exercise 4 – Fred

I hope you managed to find out some information about Fred the horse (page 119). If you did, that's great validation for you.

- Fred belongs to a lady called Caroline. He lives in Worcestershire and is kept at Caroline's house in a paddock. There are four other horses in a field next to him. Caroline also has two black Labrador dogs called Rosie and Tikka.
- Fred is a gentle horse; he enjoys being groomed and is easy to handle.
- Fred is a Dutch Warmblood. He was bred in Holland and came to the UK after weaning.
- Fred is now 19 years old; he is retired and lives out in his paddock.
- In the past, Fred was a showjumping horse, winning many prizes. He was bought by Caroline when he was seven years old, so she has owned him for 12 years.
- Ten years ago, Fred was diagnosed by his vet with sacroiliac joint disease, which affects his back and pelvis, so he has now been retired from any riding activities. Fred has previously received steroid injections from the vet for this condition and has also received Equine Bowen Therapy to help relieve his symptoms.
- In the past, Fred has also suffered from laminitis in his feet, which is a painful condition which causes inflammation in

the tissue in the foot. This is managed through his diet, so Fred has to stay in his stable in the daytime during the spring and summer months when the grass is rich.

- Fred has appeared on UK TV on ITV's *This Morning* programme, as he is a very psychic horse that made a prediction that Caroline would meet a man who was a sailor with a large scar on his leg. This came true and made the headlines.

Exercise 5 – Locating a Missing Animal

Vivienne (page 166) was lost in London.

Exercise 6 – Cindy

How much did you pick up about Cindy (page 188)?

- Cindy passed away at the age of 14.
- She was rescued when she was nine months old and taken to a dog rehoming centre in Birmingham, UK, in 1983.
- Cindy was a Jack Russell Terrier crossbreed.
- Cindy was adopted by me and my family. She was sweet and loyal, but she loved to chew things, including wooden chair legs. She would also dig holes in the garden.
- Cindy was a loving and kind-natured dog. She socialized well with other dogs and lived with a cat called Tinker.

- Cindy was good with children and very gentle.
- Cindy's best friend was a Terrier called Scamp who would regularly visit. She would become very excited when she saw him or even at the sound of his name.
- Cindy was a playful and cheeky character; she was quite vocal and would make various sounds as if she was talking verbally to members of her family.
- Cindy loved most foods, but liver and sausage was her favourite. She would also enjoy an occasional bone.
- Cindy loved to go out for walks and travel in the car; she loved swimming and would jump right into streams and rivers whenever she had the opportunity.
- When off the lead, Cindy would never wander far away; she would always turn and check your whereabouts and come back when called (unless she was swimming).
- As Cindy got older, she became blind. She remained active up until her passing, when she was put to sleep by a local vet, who advised this to be the best course of action due to her other underlying health issues.

Acknowledgements

I wish to thank:

All my family, especially my parents, Dot and Keith, my sister and brother-in-law, Angela and Derek, for all their love, support and encouragement;

My partner, Nigel, for his loyalty and for always telling me to "go for it!";

My children, Rachael, Kieran and Alice, for inspiring me to be more adventurous and for telling me, "You can do it," and my stepson, Matt, for his love and support;

My niece, Hannah, for making my hair look fabulous on TV!;

My niece, Sophie, who is the kindest soul and also a pet psychic in training;

My kind and loving aunties and uncles, who treat me more like another daughter than a niece, and my cousins who are like sisters to me. I really do have the best family, for which I am extremely grateful.

Thank you to Adam Claxton and Hayley Guest for your help and support.

Grateful thanks to Wendy Hobson, Susan Clarke, Matt Tomlinson and Beth Bishop for their excellent editing. A special mention to Naz Ahsun and Jo Lal for their support and advice in turning this book into a reality. To all my friends and clients for being open-minded enough to listen to the messages from their pets and acting upon them.

And finally, to all the animals I have had the privilege of communicating with.

Useful Resources

Below are some of my recommendations if you would like to explore the subjects covered in this book further.

Further Reading

All Pets Go to Heaven: The Spiritual Lives of the Animals We Love, Sylvia Browne (Piatkus, 2010).

The Amazing Power of Animals, Gordon Smith (Hay House UK, 2008).

Animal Spirit Guides, Dr Steven D Farmer, PhD (Hay House, 2006).

Discover Your Power Animal, Naz Ahsun (Trigger Publishing, 2021).

Dogs That Know When Their Owners Are Coming Home: And Other Unexplained Powers of Animals, Rupert Sheldrake (Arrow, 2000).

Pet Grief: How to Cope Before & After, Jackie Weaver (CreateSpace Independent Publishing Platform, 2018).

Straight from the Horse's Mouth: How to Talk to Animals and Get Answers, Amelia Kinkade (New World Library, 2005).

Angels

The Angel Mystic's Manifesting Manual: An Easy Guide to Manifesting, Amanda Tooke (Mystic Moon, 2020).

Angels in My Hair, Lorna Byrne (Arrow Revised Edition, 2010)

Connecting with the Angels Made Easy: How to See, Hear and Feel Your Angels, Kyle Gray (Hay House UK, 2018).

The Essential Manifesting Guidebook 2022: Simple Steps to Create the Life You Truly Desire, Trish McKinnley (7th Star Publishing, 2021).

The Female Archangels: Reclaim your Power with the Lost Teachings of the Divine Feminine, Claire Stone (Hay House UK, 2020).

Manifestation: The Secret, Rhonda Byrne (Simon & Schuster UK, 2006).

Super Attractor: Methods for Manifesting a Life Beyond Your Wildest Dreams, Gabrielle Bernstein (Hay House, 2021).

Talking with Angels of Love: Open Your Heart, Amanda Hart (Orion Spring, 2020).

Crystals

The Encyclopaedia of Crystals, Judy Hall (Fair Winds Press, 2013).

The Little Book of Crystals: Crystals to Attract Love, Wellbeing and Spiritual Harmony into Your Life, Judy Hall (Gala, 2016).

Healing

Animal Reiki: Using Energy to Heal the Animals in Your Life, Elizabeth Fulton and Kathleen Prasad (Ulysses Press, illustrated edition, 2020).

Chakra Healing: A Beginners Guide Self-Healing Techniques that Balance the Chakras, Margarita Alcantra (Althea Press, 2017).

Crystal Reiki Healing: The Powerhouse Therapy for Mind, Body and Spirit, Philip Permutt (CICO Books, 2020).

Self-Help

The 3 Things That Will Change Your Destiny Today!, Paul McKenna (Transworld Digital, 2017).

Answers in the Dark: Grief, Sleep and How Your Dreams Can Help You Heal, Delphi Ellis (O-Books, 2022).

The Code of the Extraordinary Mind: 10 Unconventional Laws to Redefine Your Life and Succeed on Your Own Terms, Vishen Lakhiani (Bantam Dell Publishing Group, Div of Random House, 2019).

Conquering Anxiety: Stop Worrying, Beat Stress and Feel Happy Again, The Speakmans. (Orion Spring, 2019).

The High 5 Habit: Take Control of Your Life with One Simple Habit, Mel Robbins (Hay House UK, 2021).

Leadership Edge, Pure Coaching: A Practical Guide to Becoming a Great Leader, Jan Rudge & Hayley Guest. (Compass-Publishing, 2021).

Life By Numbers: Unlock the Answers You Seek by Using the Power of 'Universal Number Attraction', Elizabeth Barber (Compass-Publishing, 2017).

Think Like a Monk: The Secret of How to Harness the Power of Positivity and Be Happy Now, Jay Shetty (Thorsons, 2020).

Oracle Card Decks

Archangel Power Tarot Cards: A 78-Card Deck and Guidebook, Radleigh Valentine (Hay House, 2018).

Messages from the Mermaids: A 44-Card Deck and Guidebook, Karen Kay (Hay House, 2020).

The Spirit Animal Oracle: A 68-Card Deck and Guidebook, Colette Baron-Reid (Hay House, 2018).

Podcasts and Radio Shows

Happy Place: Fearne Cotton chats to inspiring individuals who have either made a change in their own lives or who help people everyday to find a different way of looking at life.

Master your Mind Podcast with Marisa Peer: Marisa is a celebrity therapist who explores different topics to improve your self-development (www.marisapeer.com).

MindValley Podcast: dedicated to personal growth and self-improvement. Features leading experts and speakers in transformational thinking (www.mindvalley.com).

Psychic Beth's 'Spiritual Calling' Radio Show: Guest interviews, Psychic Development and Free Psychic and Pet Psychic Readings. Every Wednesday 6-8pm (GMT) www.pulsetalkradio.com.

Psychic Matters with Ann Theato: Ann is an international psychic medium, author and approved tutor for Tony Stockwell's Soul Space. She covers how to develop your spiritual gifts and interviews leading spiritual experts (www.anntheato.com).

Secrets for an Inspirational Life with Mimi Novic: Mimi is a bestselling author and interviews incredible people from across the globe who have inspirational and motivational stories to tell (www.miminovic.co.uk).

Social Dog Podcast by Cindie Carter: Devoted to inspiring, motivating, and educating both dog owners as well as those who love dogs.

Spiritual Resources

International Psychics Association: founded as the Australian Psychic Association in 1983, and still based in Australia (www.internationalpsychicsassociation.com).

The London Spiritual Mission: a London-based spiritualist church (www.spiritualmission.co.uk).

The Psychic Directory: this website covers worldwide information and lists about organisations, spiritual churches, psychic mediums and more from all over the globe. It has an easy-to-use search feature (www.psychic-directory.com).

Society of Novus Spiritus: Based in the USA, their website has lots of information, including where to find study groups, the New Spirit Radio Show, dream analysis and spiritual counselling classes, as well as church services (www.novus.org).

The Spirit Guides: an online directory advertising a large range of spiritual events, workshops, centres, courses, articles, podcasts and services all over the UK. You can join their newsletter to keep updated with the latest news and you can also add your own event (www.thespiritguides.co.uk).

Spiritual Events & Directory: this Australian online resource features a New Age directory of events and services, covering subjects including astrology, spiritual shops, life coaching, spiritual retreats, psychic readings and venue hire (www.spiritualeventsdirectory.com).

The Spiritualist Church of Canada: aims to promote the religion of spiritualism and its philosophies across Canada and the world. They hold regular virtual divine services and courses in spiritualism, which include the subjects of mediums and mediumship, spiritual healing, spiritualism in Canada, comparative religion, and platform etiquette and chairing (www.spiritualistchurchofcanada.com).

Pet Bereavement Resources

There are some excellent telephone bereavement services available that many people do not know exist.

- Animal Samaritans' Pet Bereavement Service (www.animalsamaritans.org.uk).
- Blue Cross: offers a Pet Bereavement Service (www.bluecross.org.uk). Also offers a Pet Bereavement Training Course (email pbsstraining@bluecross.org.uk).
- Cats Protection's "Paws to Listen" service (www.cats.org.uk).
- The Dogs Trust: offers a service called "Canine Care Card", where if the owner becomes ill or passes away, The Dogs Trust will look after the dog and help them find a new home (www.dogstrust.org.uk).
- EASE Pet Loss Support Services (www.ease-animals.org.uk).
- Rainbows Bridge: this USA-based site is a virtual memorial home and grief-support community. (www.rainbowsbridge.com).
- Pets and People: this Australia-based site is a support network for grieving pet owners. They have a 24-hour pet loss support line – please note there may be a charge for this service (Australia: 1300 431 450, NZ: 0800 114 421, www.petsandpeople.com.au).

Lost or Missing Pet Advice

- Dog Lost: the UK's largest free lost and found service (www.doglost.co.uk).
- Lost Pet Finders: Australia's largest lost and found service, recognised by vets, councils and volunteer organisations (www.lostpetfinders.com.au).
- Paw Boost: a resource site where you can add your missing pet to their database, which contains free tools such as printing flyers and alerting the "Rescue Squad" (www.pawboost.com).
- Pet FBI: a free database and information centre for lost and found pets in USA, Puerto Rico and the Virgin Islands (www.petfbi.org).

Legislation around Setting Up Your Own Business

UK

For information on UK legislation, you can refer to www.legislation.gov.uk. The Fraudulent Mediums Act 1951 England and Wales replaced the Witchcraft Act 1735 and in turn repealed on 26 March 2008.

USA

In the USA, laws can vary state to state. For example, Annapolis, Maryland, requires psychics to undergo a police background check and obtain a licence. Similarly, Salem, Massachusetts, requires background checks for psychics and even caps the number allowed in town (information taken from www.hg.org/legal-articles/are-there-any-laws-that-regulate-psychics-31845). You should carefully consult your state's laws and requirements.

Australia

If you're in Australia you should check your state laws. There is a degree of self-regulation: the International Psychics Association has its own code of ethics. Consumer Affairs Victoria also advises that consumers are protected by the Fair Trading Act 1999 (information taken from www.findlaw.com.au).

Mental Health Advice

UK

- Claxton Coaching: Adam Claxton coaches people to be the best version of themselves and specializes in men's mental health (www.claxtoncoaching.com).
- Mind: www.mind.org.uk.
- Samaritans: UK telephone: 116123, www.samaritans.org.
- Scottish Association for Mental Health (SAMH): www.samh.org.uk

USA

- Mental Health America: www.mhanational.org
- National Institute of Mental Health: www.nimh.nih.gov

Canada

- Canadian Mental Health Association: cmha.ca
- Crisis Service Canada: www.ementalhealth.ca

Australia and New Zealand

- Mental Health Australia: mhaustralia.org
- Mental Health Foundation of New Zealand: www.mentalhealth.org.nz

Further Training

- Canine massage therapy: www.k9-massage.co.uk
- Equine therapy: www.equineassitedtherapyaustrailia.com, www leapequine.com, www.equinetherapy.center
- Online counselling courses: www.learndirect.com
- TTouch Training: www.ttouchtraining.co.uk; www.ttouch.com

Reiki Healing and Training

Reiki training can be done in person or there are online courses. To find a teacher or practitioner in your area, visit www.reiki.org.

Crystal Therapy

There are online and in-person classes available to become a crystal therapist through the following links:

- UK: www.britishacademyofcrystalhealing.co.uk
- USA: www.energyhealingschoolny.com
- Australia: www.naturalenergies.com.au

Dog Yoga

"Doga" is a human yoga practice that helps support the natural bond between a person and their dog. There are classes available on YouTube (www.dogayoga.fit).

About Us

Welbeck Balance is dedicated to changing lives.
Our mission is to deliver life-enhancing books to help improve your wellbeing so that you can live with greater clarity and meaning, wherever you are on life's journey.

Welbeck Balance is part of the Welbeck Publishing Group – a globally recognized, independent publisher based in London. Welbeck are renowned for our innovative ideas, for our production values and for developing long-lasting content. Our books have been translated into over 30 languages in more than 60 countries around the world.

If you love books, then join the club and sign up to our newsletter for exclusive offers, extracts, author interviews and more information.

To find out more and sign up, visit:

www.welbeckpublishing.com

welbeckpublish
welbeckpublish
welbeckuk